**Connecting Reading and Writing in
Second Language Writing Instruction**

Michigan Series on Teaching Multilingual Writers

Series Editors

**Diane Belcher (Georgia State University) and
Jun Liu (University of Arizona)**

Available titles in the series

Connecting Reading and Writing in Second Language Writing Instruction

Alan Hirvela
Ohio State University

Michigan Series on Teaching Multilingual Writers

THE UNIVERSITY OF MICHIGAN PRESS
Ann Arbor

Copyright © by the University of Michigan 2004
All rights reserved
Published in the United States of America by
The University of Michigan Press
Manufactured in the United States of America
∞ Printed on acid-free paper

2007   2006   2005   2004   4   3   2   1

A CIP catalog record for this book is available from the British Library.

Library of Congress Cataloging-in-Publication Data

Hirvela, Alan.
    Connecting reading and writing in second language writing
instruction / Alan Hirvela.
        p.   cm. — (Michigan series on teaching multilingual writers)
    Includes bibliographical references and index.
    ISBN 0-472-08918-8 (pbk. : alk. paper)
    1. Language and languages—Study and teaching.   2. Rhetoric—
Study and teaching.   3. Reading.   4. Second language acquisition.
I. Title.   II. Series.

P53.27.H57   2004
418′.0071—dc22

                                            2004051766

Figures on pages 29 and 30 are from R. J. Tierney (1992), Ongoing research
and new directions. In J. W. Irwin & M. A. Doyle (Eds.), *Reading/writing
connections: Learning from research* (pp. 246–259). Newark, DE: International Reading Association. Reprinted with permission of Robert J. Tierney
and the International Reading Association. All rights reserved.

For Michael Moore, who "speaks truth to power" so courageously and eloquently

Acknowledgments

I'm indebted to many people for their help and support before and during this project.

I'd like to thank Diane Belcher and Jun Liu, editors of the Michigan Series on Teaching Multilingual Writers, for the opportunity to write this book, with special appreciation to Diane for her wonderful generosity and collegiality over the years we've worked together. I'm also extremely grateful to Kelly Sippell and Christina Milton at the University of Michigan Press for their great patience, understanding, and assistance.

Thanks also to George Newell and to my colleagues and students in ESL Composition and Foreign/Second Language Education at Ohio State University for creating an environment that helped make the writing of this book possible.

Thanks, too, to my longtime friends and former colleagues Jim Drummond, Herb Pierson, and Eva Law, who provided encouragement from afar, and to my mentor and friend from my Chinese University days, Joe Boyle, for long ago pointing me in the direction that this book came from.

Finally, I'd like to express my love and gratitude to my wife, Soonei, and my family for their encouragement and support throughout this project. And I'd like to pay tribute to the memory of my father and my brother, who are never forgotten.

Contents

Series Foreword

There are a number of very compelling reasons for including a book on reading-writing connections in a series such as ours, which is devoted to helping teachers of multilingual writers. Not least of these is the current state of knowledge of the synergistic relationship of the reading and writing processes. We have been aware for several decades now of the cognitive advantages of linking reading and writing activities. There are probably few intensive English programs or secondary/postsecondary ESL composition or "bridge" classes these days that do not make some attempt to integrate these literacy skills in their curricula. Moving from a cognitive to a more social-epistemic vantage point, we see that, in addition to the learning strategy advantages, there are real-world, or discourse community, motivations for connecting reading and writing pedagogically. It is difficult to find a community, academic or otherwise, in which whatever writing is accomplished is not to some extent "text responsible prose" (Leki and Carson, 1997)—that is, responsive to information gleaned from reading, whether from print or electronic sources. Multilingual writers unprepared for such community expectations may find the doors to membership in the particular literacy club (Smith, 1987) they seek to join rather hard to open.

There may not be many L2 literacy instructors, with the exception of those new to the field, who still need to be persuaded of the validity of the preceding arguments, yet many may feel that they are indeed in need of the type of guidance in the optimal blending of reading-writing instruction that Alan Hirvela provides in *Connecting Reading and Writing in Second Language Writing Instruction.* As Hirvela points out (this volume), there are surprisingly few relevant resources available in the professional L2 literature. The Carson and Leki (1993) and Belcher and Hirvela (2001) anthologies of scholarly articles are no doubt useful resources, but neither provides the sustained, cohesive view of integrated L2 reading-writing pedagogy with practitioners foremost in mind that can be found in *Connecting Reading and Writing*. Hirvela's extensive knowledge of both L1 and L2 reading-writing research (the latter of which he himself has impressively contributed to), his talent for translating theoretical abstractions into easy-to-understand terms, and his own grounding in L2 classroom experience, as one who taught ESL for many years and currently teaches TESOL graduate students, makes him especially well suited to the task he has set for himself in this book. From firsthand experience, he understands how to convert research and theory into effective classroom practice and how to help others appreciate the value of doing so. Current practitioners as well as those in training and their faculty mentors will likely especially value the scope of Hirvela's text:

- the contextualization and rationale building of the historical and theoretical overviews
- the alternating and ultimately reinforcing perspectives of writing in support of reading and reading in the service of writing
- the timely, much needed look at the reading-writing-technology interface
- the guidance provided for text and task selection as well as implementation of particular assignments or activities for differing levels of proficiency
- and, finally, the road map to professional enrichment offered in this volume's extensive bibliography of reading-writing literature compiled with an eye toward the needs of teachers of multilingual learners

It will be readily apparent to readers of this volume that voices that should be heard in a book such as this are present throughout—voices not only from L1 and L2 literacy research circles but also from the classroom, including Hirvela's own teacher-researcher voice and student voices, that, though not immediately audible, are indirectly "heard" through an array of model teacher-student literacy task interactions. Teachers of L2 literacy who are committed to or simply interested in efficaciously connecting reading and writing instruction should feel that this is a book that speaks to and for them.

References

Belcher, D., and Hirvela, A. (Eds.). (2001). *Linking literacies: Perspectives on L2 reading-writing connections.* Ann Arbor: University of Michigan Press.

Carson, J. G., and Leki, I. (Eds.). (1993). *Reading in the composition classroom: Second language perspectives.* Boston: Heinle and Heinle.

Leki, I., and Carson, J. (1997). "Completely different worlds": EAP and the writing experiences of ESL students in university courses. *TESOL Quarterly, 31,* 39–69.

Smith, F. (1987). *Joining the literacy club.* Portsmouth, NH: Heinemann.

Diane Belcher,
Georgia State University

Jun Liu,
University of Arizona

Introduction

An illuminating experience in the professional lives of many L2 writing teachers is the recognition that their students' difficulties while writing in the L2 are not necessarily or not predominantly writing problems per se. Upon closer examination, they can often be traced to problems in reading. At the postsecondary level especially, where, as Carson and Leki (1993a) note, "reading can be, and in academic settings nearly always is, the basis for writing" (p. 1), students' ability to write is heavily dependent on and influenced by their ability to read, and vice versa. For example, academic writing often requires incorporating material from source texts—statistics, ideas, quotations, paraphrases, and so forth—into written texts. Students who read well know where to locate and how to identify the most relevant content in the source texts, and that information is then transferred to their writing. If the writing that follows reading is poor, the problem may be in ineffective reading that failed to properly access necessary source text information, not in writing ability itself. As such, attention needs to be paid to how students composing from such sources of information are reading those sources.

When we begin to investigate a situation like that and concentrate on the reading, we may find that the core problem is in fact the reader's inability to use writing to shape reading. To read well, the student needs to know where to look for information and how to identify it as relevant or useful. Where does such knowledge come from? Our answer in this book is that it comes in part from writing; that is, the knowledge necessary to obtain such material may come at least in part from what students know about texts as writers. That knowledge tells them how, rhetorically and linguistically, texts in the target language function, just as a road map tells a driver how to reach Point B from Point A. Thus, their writing knowledge informs their ability to read.

Conversely, exposure to texts through reading has probably contributed to their acquisition of understanding about writing and those features that constitute writing: the rhetorical strategies, cohesive devices, and other tools of writing that writers use to present their ideas. Acquiring such knowledge from reading should eventually assist students while writing by equipping them with helpful knowledge of writing strategies and techniques. And it should, in turn, assist reading by providing some of the equipment necessary to process texts.

We see, then, that there are complex ways in which reading and writing interact. What we know about reading comes partly from writing, and what we know about writing comes partly from reading. It is this kind of scenario that has inspired such oft-made comments as "good writers are good readers" and "good readers are good writers." On the other hand, bad writers may be bad readers, in that they are unable, as readers, to successfully process or make use of source texts, leaving them ill prepared for the act of writing about those texts because their reading has not effectively informed their writing.

Though L2 writing instructors may intuitively sense that there are important connections between the acts of reading and writing as they arrive at the understanding just described, they are not necessarily prepared to fully appreciate or recognize the various relationships that exist between the two skills, such as the key idea that writing and reading depend on many of the same composing processes. For one thing, it's easy to conceptualize the writing course as just that: a course about *writing*. As Kroll (1993), among others, has pointed out, reading has traditionally been seen as a skill to be taught separately from writing, as well as something students are somehow expected to already know about when they reach the writing course. Teaching reading in a writing course may seem like an odd idea, if not an entirely unnecessary one. It may also be the case that L2 writing teachers feel ill prepared to teach reading, especially in connection with writing. How many have actually been taught to teach the two skills together? They may also feel that teaching writing is hard enough as it is and that adding reading to the equation will make the task too difficult to perform well.

Then there's the time factor. Writing classes are busy places with no room to spare; where will pedagogical space be found to incorporate reading into the mix? That's a question many teachers are likely to ask—even if they accept the belief that discussing reading with writing is a good idea.

A very different kind of problem we need to consider is that our notions of reading and writing may be changing and, indeed, may need to be changed. Historically speaking, *reading* meant reading print or hard copy sources: books, newspapers, magazines, and so forth. And that, in turn, meant reading in a *linear* way: start from the beginning and work systematically to the end. *Writing* meant using a pen or pencil or typewriter to record one's words. Today, however, we can no longer assume that these are the technologies students use when they read and write. Nowadays we need to account for online reading and writing, as students' encounters with reading and writing may well be based in cyberspace. It is more and more the case that students turn to the Internet for sources of information and to a computer to write their essays. What, then, does it mean to say that we *read,* for instance, a hypertext document with all its links and its nonlinear nature (where there is no clear-cut beginning, middle, or ending)? What does the word *write* mean when it involves, say, authoring a web page or home page? The most reasonable answer to these questions is that terms like *reading* and *writing* don't necessarily mean what they once did; one does not *read* or *write* a hypertext the way she or he reads articles and writes essays. And yet reading and writing are taking place. Students are still *composing* meaning. But how the composing processes are enacted when the textual environments they take place within are electronic in nature may vary considerably from conventional acts of print-based reading and writing.

The preceding questions are important ones for us because

we live increasingly in a world of electronic or online literacy, and the academic work our students perform in many courses may involve electronically based reading and writing. That being so, they need our help in learning how to successfully complete these tasks—tasks that are still in the process of being defined and understood because of (a) the relative newness of the world of electronic literacy and (b) the dynamic, ever changing nature of that world as technology undergoes constant upgrades. Meanwhile, students still require the ability to read and write as those skills have long been practiced, that is, in the world of print literacy. Thus, we, as L2 writing teachers, find ourselves in a complex in-between time with respect to second language literacy, one in which we may need to teach both print and screen or online literacy skills.

At present, then, L2 writing teachers are faced with perhaps unprecedented challenges as we straddle the worlds of print and electronic literacy and attempt to link reading and writing within these domains. At the same time, though, we face unprecedented opportunities as well. Because of advances in technology in particular—for example, the much easier access to computers than in the past and the increasingly easy access to an ever richer Internet—our students can *do* more with reading and writing than was possible in the past.

The primary purpose of this book is to bridge the past, present, and future by looking closely at what we know about reading and writing connections and what we, as teachers, can do with that knowledge as we engage this complicated interface between old and new ways of reading and writing. The book tries to put past and present understandings of reading-writing connections into perspectives that will serve the interests of a wide range of practitioners and future practitioners: those who have not yet embraced the notion of close links between reading and writing, those who are still learning about those links and wish to know more, and those who are well acquainted with such links and seek to refresh and perhaps expand their understanding of them. This is especially important as we engage the academic literacy demands of the

21st century and must find ways to realign L2 writing instruction in response to those demands.

Through this book's combined focus on important theories, research findings, and classroom practices related to L2 (as well as L1) reading-writing connections, it is hoped that readers will gain a solid footing in this vital area of L2 teaching and feel empowered to construct their own reading-writing classes relative to their own needs and demands as teachers. Exposure to the theories, research, and practice discussed in this book should provide readers with a clear sense of the pedagogical options available to them and thus better prepare them to make wise choices for their own instructional activity. The book has been written so as to supply readers with a good working foundation in reading-writing relationships and a host of ideas and suggestions for actual classroom practice.

Wherever it is that writing is taught—in a K–12 setting, a community college, or a four-year college or university—there are ways in which reading can be linked to writing and assist in the development of writing skills. How the two skills are integrated in terms of approaches, materials, and assessment may vary according to the particular educational setting involved and the needs of the students in that location. What K–12 students need in terms of reading and writing will certainly differ from the requirements or expectations facing, say, community college students. Likewise, teachers should account for whether their students are immigrants—that is, Generation 1.5—students (principally in K–12 schools and to some extent at community colleges) or so-called visa students (those who have come from overseas for the sole purpose of college-level study). However, while it is necessary to consider how the concepts and approaches discussed in this book apply in these different contexts, it should be understood that the book lays out a core foundation of notions and techniques concerning reading-writing relations that can serve as a starting point for any writing instruction that seeks to link reading and writing.

It should also be understood that the reading-writing connections theme of this book is not meant to suggest that there are never good reasons to teach writing and reading separately from each other. Each of these skills has its own unique characteristics, and some circumstances might well demand that students focus on just one of the skills. The book puts forth the notion of reading-writing connections as a construct deserving primary, but not exclusive, consideration in the design of a second language writing course.

Finally, while the book is aimed at those who teach second language writers, it draws heavily on ideas and research provided by those who work with students of writing whose native language is English, that is, first language writers, and its core concepts are applicable in courses aimed at those students as well. It can also be adapted to courses featuring a mix of nonnative and native speakers of English. Here, again, some adaptations to fit local circumstances may be in order, but the book can be used by anyone who teaches writing.

Chapter 1 creates a framework for the chapters that follow by reviewing major conceptualizations of reading-writing connections, particularly in the L2 context. This chapter provides a sense of the historical and thematic development of the field of reading-writing relations.

Chapter 2 introduces a focus not yet fully articulated in the L2 reading-writing relationships literature: *reader-response theory*. In the domain of reading-writing connections work, there is an as yet underdeveloped view or emphasis on L2 students' experiences as readers within writing contexts. The thesis of this chapter is that work in the L2 reading-writing classroom can be enriched by constructing or observing students first as *readers* and that reader-response theory provides the best mechanism by which to privilege students' composing activities as readers and to link those activities to writing. The chapter briefly examines the main tenets of reader-response theory and shows how they can be used to further our understanding of relationships between reading and writing in L2 writing instruction. Applications of a reader-response approach in a high school and a college setting are provided.

Chapter 3 looks in depth at an important dimension of reading-writing connections: the use of writing *for* reading. This is one of the major areas in which reading-writing relations have been explored in both research and practice. It is believed that if students struggle with reading (L1 or L2), various types of writing can prove invaluable in enhancing understanding and appreciation of a text and therefore building reading ability. A good case in point is summary writing. While writing a summary, students undertake close, focused reading of a text and thus learn to engage the text more meaningfully or skillfully as a reader. Chapter 3 shows how certain uses of writing for primarily reading-based purposes contribute to L2 literacy acquisition, with a particular focus on developing L2 reading ability.

Chapter 4 is in essence an extension of Chapter 3, but with a reverse in focus. Here the emphasis is on reading *for* writing—that is, acts of reading geared not toward baseline comprehension of a text or improving reading skills but, rather, toward producing more informed and effective writing. The link to Chapter 3 comes partly in the examination of the same kinds of literacy-building activities—for example, summarizing, synthesizing, quoting, and paraphrasing. This time, though, they're portrayed as acts beginning in reading and leading to writing, rather than beginning in writing and leading back to reading (as in Chap. 3).

Chapter 5 adds depth to the previous three chapters by focusing more extensively on pedagogical possibilities related to the reading-writing emphases of those chapters. This is achieved by presenting several major models of reading-writing connections and discussing ways in which they relate to the reading-writing approaches described in Chapters 2–4. The chapter sheds light on how to employ those approaches. The practical, classroom-based orientation of this chapter should prove especially helpful to readers.

It is important to note from the start that the three primary frameworks for or modes of reading-writing connections presented in this book—*reader response, writing to read,* and *reading to write*—apply equally to both the print and electronic text domains of reading and writing. How they are enacted may change because of inherent differences in the ways people read and write in the print and electronic worlds, but as teachers we can work from a response-based, writing-to-read, or reading-to-write orientation in both of these textual environments.

A recurring theme in the current professional literature and at conferences is the need to help L2 writers acquire an appropriate level of academic literacy knowledge and ability. Reading and writing and the ways in which they interact in academic settings are crucial elements in this acquisition. The approach taken in this book is intended to assist L2 writing instructors and teachers-in-training in understanding the issues and challenges they face in the process of trying to develop students' L2 literacy skills, both print and electronically based, and in establishing the important instructional link between reading and writing that may still be lacking in many classrooms. While to some teachers the idea of treating reading and writing together may seem not only logical but unavoidable, it might be the case that they have yet to find meaningful ways of connecting the skills. Meanwhile, many teachers may be perpetuating the traditional skills separation model of L2 teaching in which reading and writing are taught independently of each other. This book is intended to help teachers and teachers-to-be in all of these categories by reviewing what we currently know about reading-writing connections and discussing how we can best facilitate those connections.

Chapter 1

An Overview of
Reading-Writing Connections

We believe that at the heart of understanding reading and writing connections one must begin to view reading and writing as essentially similar processes of meaning construction. Both are acts of composing. (Tierney & Pearson, 1983, p. 568)

This quotation, from the seminal article "Toward a Composing Model of Reading" in a landmark issue of the journal *Language Arts* (which contained several influential articles about reading-writing connections), represents an ideal starting point for this book. In particular, the statement that "both [reading and writing] are acts of composing" captures the essence of what *Connecting Reading and Writing* is about.

What we need to understand about the Tierney and Pearson quote is the departure from conventional thinking and teaching practice it represented at the time of its publication. While it was obvious that writing is an act of composing, it wasn't common in 1983 to think of reading in such terms. Then, reading was generally conceptualized as a passive act of *decoding meaning and information* in accordance with the intentions of the author of a text. Furthermore, it was common practice then to teach reading separately from writing because of the way in which the two skills were divided: writing as an active skill and reading as a passive one.

Let me now make a confession that also points out the desirability of beginning with what Tierney and Pearson said. My career as a writing teacher began in the 1970s in a community college setting where I was teaching native speakers of English. As a writing teacher, I thought only of writing; it didn't occur to me that reading could be factored heavily into the writing equation, except in the sense of providing models of what essays should look like. My hope, like that of probably most writing instructors at the time, was that students would basically imitate the rhetorical structures of the models. Though this use of source texts was in fact an act connecting reading and writing, with reading being used to support or shape writing, it didn't occur to me to construct the use of model essays as an activity linking reading and writing. My focus was on the writing that would be produced; reading was secondary to that process. Here, again, I was following commonly established practice and belief: writing teachers teach writing, and reading teachers teach reading. Like my colleagues at the time, that's the way I thought about writing instruction, and that's how I was taught to think. Nothing in my graduate school training had encouraged a conscious linking of reading and writing.

It wasn't until the 1980s, when I was teaching in Hong Kong and working with L2 writers, that I began to wonder about possible connections between writing and reading. At the time, I was assigning a fair amount of reading that the students were supposed to write about in various ways. As I saw many of my students struggling with the essays they were writing, I was thinking, as I had in the 1970s, that they were experiencing writing problems (as well as language-related difficulties). And then, for one particular assignment that was proving problematic, I asked the students to bring their copies of the assigned readings to their writing conferences with me. We began looking at them to find ways to move material from the readings to the essays being written. That's when I became more aware of the reading problems many of the students were having and when I recognized, in a half-formed way, that some of the writing difficulties I had observed were in fact *reading* difficulties. Or, to be more accurate, they were *composing* difficulties. Locked into the language of the texts at the word and sentence level, many of the students were engaged in bottom-up reading that involved mechanical decoding of the texts.

There was no real effort to link the texts to what the students were writing; they were too busy checking their dictionaries to figure out what the words in the texts meant. And I was equally busy reinforcing that kind of reading behavior by not talking at all about the reading side of writing. Indeed, I was still separating reading from writing, as if the two acts had to take place at separate times under separate circumstances. I was also still assuming that the reading side of the writing assignments took care of itself; my job was to teach the writing.

Thankfully, we gradually began spending more time in class discussing the readings, in the context of what they meant with respect to the writing the students were doing. Soon we were talking about effective reading strategies, but not strategies aimed strictly at comprehension of the texts. Instead, and without a conscious decision on my part to do so, we somehow were looking more and more at reading as it related to writing. What we were doing, in essence, was what Tierney and Pearson described in the quote at the beginning of this chapter: we were talking about reading as an act of *composing* (though we didn't use that term at the time). As we talked about the students' writing summaries of the assigned readings, for example, we began looking more carefully at how they could use the same rhetorical structures encountered in their reading of the assigned texts in their writing. And that led us to looking at how they could use their knowledge of conventions of writing to make better sense of their reading in the context of knowing *what to look for* in their reading and *where to find it,* as in the case of such writing staples as thesis statements and topic sentences. Slowly but surely, then, we were encountering similarities in how one reads and writes—that is, how the same architectures of expression apply in both domains. In our own simple and uninformed way, we were portraying the actions of readers and writers in the ways Tierney and Pearson described.

Since that time, I have been convinced, like many other L2 writing teachers, that one of the best ways to improve writing is to improve reading, and vice versa; and that in the writing classroom, a lesson about writing is a lesson about reading, and vice versa. That leads to a third conviction: it makes more sense to include discussion of reading in the writing class than to treat the two skills separately.

Those convictions capture some of the core beliefs in the field of reading-writing connections. There are, however, numerous ways to conceptualize and examine how reading and writing overlap, and the purpose of this opening chapter is to review the major perspectives that have guided the development of the field of reading-writing connections. Using a combined thematic-chronological approach, we'll track the evolution of the notion of reading-writing relationships so as to create a foundation from which to operate in reading the remaining chapters of this book. To know and understand where the field stands now, we need to know how it got there.

Major Constructions of Reading-Writing Connections

In this section, we're going to briefly review the principal themes that have directed and defined the growth of the field of reading-writing connections. This will be done by looking at a number of significant examinations of reading-writing connections so as to draw attention to what the authors in this field saw as the key configurations of reading-writing relationships. In this way we'll be able to track, thematically, the foundations of this field.

Stotsky (1983) provided the first major review of reading-writing scholarship. Although such scholarship dates back to the beginning of the 20th century, Stotsky was struck by what she called "the relative paucity of research on the interrelation of two major components [reading and writing] of literacy" (p. 627). By the early '80s, then, a clear picture of reading-writing connections had not yet emerged.

In her review, Stotsky focused on three themes or focuses of research:

1. Correlational studies
2. Studies examining the influence of writing on reading
3. Studies examining the influence of reading on writing

The correlational studies looked at possible relationships between reading ability or achievement and writing ability, while the other two areas of her review examined what has been the primary domain of interest in work linking reading and writing: the role of one of the skills in supporting the development of the other. This emphasis on the "support role" of reading and writing will be explored in greater detail in Chapters 3 and 4. With respect to this view of reading-writing relations, as Grabe and Kaplan (1996) have observed more recently: "Reading and writing are reciprocal activities; the outcome of a reading activity can serve as input for writing, and writing can lead a student to further reading resources" (p. 297). The conclusions Stotsky reported played an important role in further development of the reading-writing connections field in terms of both research and classroom practice. As Stotsky reported: "To summarize briefly, the correlational studies show almost consistently that better writers tend to be better readers (of their own writing as well as of other reading material), that better writers tend to read more than poorer writers, and that better readers tend to produce more syntactically mature writing than poorer readers" (p. 636). With respect to the explorations of the influence of one skill on the other, Stotsky reported mixed results. The use of writing exercises or activities to enhance reading (e.g., summaries) showed positive results, while efforts to link reading instruction to writing showed no meaningful effects. Reading *experience,* as opposed to direct reading instruction, was more likely to improve writing ability. With respect to materials used for reading-writing purposes, literary texts had the most positive effects on writing.

The next major report is Tierney and Shanahan's (1991) comprehensive review of reading-writing literature. This review reflects significant changes in the directions reading-writing connections research (and pedagogy) had taken, as is suggested by the title itself: "Research on the Reading-Writing Relationship: Interactions, Transactions, and Outcomes." As they explained in comparing earlier research (1970s) with more recent research (1980s), "In terms of methodology, research on reading and writing has moved beyond comparing global measures of reading with global measures of writing to consider their underlying constructs and the ongoing thinking that readers and writers pursue" (p. 274). This is reflected in their focus on the "interactions" and "transactions" mentioned earlier. We also see this in the primary areas of discussion in their review:

1. What do reading and writing share?
2. How do readers and writers transact with one another?
3. What do readers and writers learn when reading and writing are connected?

Their introduction to these three primary areas of concentration reflects the changing tides of reading-writing research:

The first topic addresses the nature of and extent to which reading and writing involve similar, shared, and overlapping linguistic, cognitive, or social resources. The second topic considers how readers and writers transact with one another as they negotiate the making of meaning. The third topic explores the thinking and learning that occurs as learners shift back and forth from reading to writing according to goals they pursue in different subject areas such as science, social studies, and literature. (p. 246)

Here we see a shift to interest in what happens *within* readers and writers as they move between reading and writing—that is, the cognitive dimensions of reading and writing—as well as in the outside influences (what Tierney and Shanahan called "social resources") affecting reading and writing. Also of particular note is the direction reflected in Tierney and Shanahan's third topic: the use of reading and writing to enhance thinking and learning in a variety of school subjects.

The conclusion of Tierney and Shanahan in 1991 is also worth noting in terms of reflecting, thematically, the state of reading-writing relations at that point in time: "We believe strongly that, in our society, at this point in history, reading and writing, to be understood and appreciated fully, should be viewed together, learned together, and used together" (p. 275).

Also in 1991, a review by Reinking and Bridwell-Bowles looked at the role of technology in the context of reading-writing connections and, in the process, provided one of the first in-depth examinations of the impact of computers on reading and writing as related processes and skills (which will be examined in Chapter 5). Reinking and Bridwell-Bowles focused on two themes:

1. The use of computers in reading and writing instruction
2. Comparisons of electronic and conventional texts

What's important here, thematically, is that we recognize the value in configuring technology, in the form of computers, in the treatment of reading and writing. Researchers and teachers were no longer focusing strictly on the print texts that had traditionally been the center of literacy teaching and research. Instead, there was a shift from a print culture to what we can call a "screen culture," in which reading and writing are increasingly enacted in the environment of a computer screen rather than the established world of hard copies or print texts. The research by Reinking and Bridwell-Bowles shows, for example, how the use of computers in reading and writing instruction was increasingly reflected in writing and reading textbooks, with chapters or larger sections of such texts devoted to this new area of reading-writing pedagogy. On the other hand, the focus at the time was generally on employing computers in reading instruction *or* writing instruction, rather than in the joint format that constitutes the heart of reading-writing connections pedagogy. Still, a role for the computer in literacy instruction was now being acknowledged, and, as the focus of the second section of their research suggests, looking at similarities and differences between electronic and traditional print texts—both those written by students and those read by them—was recognized as an important dimension of reading-writing instruction.

Tierney (1992), in another early '90s review ("Ongoing Research and New Directions"), also acknowledged the increasing role technology was playing in reading-writing instruction and research, and, at the same time, he captured the widening scope of interest in reading-writing relationships, as a look at his major areas of coverage makes clear:

- Intertextuality and integration
- Dynamic, complex, and situation-based thinking
- Multimedia and multilayered learning
- Assessment: new and better alternatives
- Reconceptualizing literacy
- Alternative assessment possibilities
- A pedagogy for empowerment

Here there is evidence of a much more complex and wide-ranging portrayal of the themes of the world of reading-writing connections than was evident in Stotsky (1983). While there was still considerable interest in the use of reading to support writing (and vice versa) and on the impact of ability in one skill on the other, a much richer and deeper context for the study and teaching of reading-writing connections was clearly emerging. With respect to "intertextuality and integration," for example, Tierney (1992) was reporting on the shift in interest from students' joint reading and writing involving a single source text to work with multiple texts, as in the case of synthesis writing, where writers must draw together, in a coherent and directive way, important insights and information from a variety of source texts. "Dynamic, complex, and situation-based thinking" reflected the developing belief in the idea that "the thinking associated with reading and writing is both dynamic and complex. The nature of thinking is apt to vary depending on changes in the learner's purposes, emerging understanding, and the context for learning, as well as the content being addressed" (p. 252). In other words, like with the shift in interest to reading and writing based on multiple source texts, there was a belief that teachers and researchers needed to avoid a narrowly defined construct of reading and writing that failed to account for the various contexts affecting reading and writing. The other themes just mentioned centered on the need to account for technology's impact on reading-writing relations, including in the multiple source text context already discussed; the importance of looking for new ways of assessing students' reading and writing to account for the widening dimensions of such activities (e.g., the use of portfolios); and the need to create better definitions of what it means to be literate, given the influences on reading and writing discussed in the other sections of the review. Meanwhile, with respect to "a pedagogy for empowerment," Tierney discussed the importance of examining moral and political dimensions of what takes place in the reading-writing classroom, such as the selection of texts used for reading-writing activities. Here he noted in particular

> the ways literacy instruction is used to subjugate and indoctrinate: the extent to which teachers control the floor and define "rightness" and "wrongness"; the prescribed reading material that is devoted to mainstream experiences; the neglect of cultural diversity; testing practices that support standardization rather than variation; promotion and retention practices that inhibit rather than encourage learning. (p. 257)

In other words, there must be accounting for "the sociopolitical dimensions of literacy" (Tierney, 1992, p. 258) if reading-writing instruction is to move beyond a restricted notion of literacy teaching as instilling basic reading and writing skills to one that encompasses the real purposes for which students will read and write, the accompanying skills needed to achieve those purposes, and the influence of social forces on how we learn to read and write and on how we conceptualize those activities.

The constructions and themes of reading-writing connections reviewed thus far have been centered on reading and writing within the L1, or native language, context. We'll look at one more of those and then briefly explore a few portrayals of L2 reading-writing connections.

In her recent (1998) reading-writing relations review, Nelson once again demonstrates the widening scope of themes emerging in the world of reading-writing connections. First, she discusses three general frameworks in which we can explore reading-writing connections: "the 'post' critique," "the communication revolution," and "the social constructionist turn." The first of these refers to postmodern or poststructuralist views in which intertextuality takes center stage, that is, "interconnections among texts," as opposed to treating texts individually and separately from each other. Furthermore, she says, "before the 'post' critique became so pervasive, reading was viewed as a different process from composing. Now we are beginning to see how both work together in hybrid acts of literacy." She also notes that this critique allows for the breaking apart of dichotomies "that have been so much a part of our discourse, such as process/product, author/audience, social/cognitive, narrative/expository, and orality/literacy." The "communication revolution" refers to the impact of technology on reading and writing. Here, she says, "of particular theoretical interest to literacy educators is hypertext, a system of interlinked textual units—texts or portions of texts—through which a reader can move" (p. 269). With respect to the "social constructivist turn," she discusses the shift in interest from individual readers and writers operating in isolation to the larger social contexts in which reading and writing occur and that influence that reading and writing.

Working within these three frameworks, Nelson examines reading-writing connections within the following thematic domains:

- Literacies as well as literacy
- Authorship as collaboration
- Texts without borders
- Permeable boundaries between reading and writing
- Identity as community

These thematic constructs once again illustrate how much interest in reading-writing connections has shifted in comparison to the work reviewed by Stotsky in 1983 and how fluid or dynamic this field is. With these themes, Nelson captures notions that now serve as major areas of concentration in reading-writing scholarship and pedagogy. In her discussion of the first of these, *literacies as well as literacy,* she demonstrates how literacy scholars are now interested in the different kinds of literacy people may experience (e.g., workplace, academic, computer) and in how, as she says, "people acquire multiple literacies over their lifetimes" (p. 274). This change from a singular to a plural view of literacy has significant implications for how we teach and research reading and writing. The next theme, *authorship as collaboration,* draws upon the just-described areas of intertextuality and social constructivism and shakes reading and writing free from the long-standing idea of a text belonging to one person, as if there were no influences on the act of composing. By looking at "authorship as collaboration," she says, teachers and researchers can account for wide-ranging interaction between readers and writers in such common classroom practices as peer review, where the revision that takes place in the act of composing is no longer the intellectual property of one author; instead, the emerging text is drawn from a variety of sources.

The notion of *texts without borders* also draws heavily on the core notion of intertextuality. As Nelson explains, "Texts— essays, stories, jokes, newspaper articles, conversations, research reports—are produced within a context of other texts. When composing, writers draw from experiences they have with other texts, and the writings they produce reflect those experiences" (pp. 276–277). In other words, we have to enlarge our notion of what a term like *text* means. Finally, her discussion of *permeable boundaries between reading and writing* returns to traditional themes in reading-writing connections— reading and writing as joint acts of composing—with a greater emphasis on the overlapping nature of the two activities. In the current construction, she explains:

> Now there is an awareness that many acts of literacy are hybrid in nature, in that they involve both composing and

comprehending. In these hybrid acts the two processes cannot be neatly separated at some point where one stops and the other starts. . . . In such acts, reading and writing processes tend to blur and a person is in two roles concurrently—a reader building meaning from a text and a writer building meaning for a text. (p. 279)

At this point, we have seen, in terms of major themes and constructions, the evolution of perspectives on reading-writing connections as they relate to native speakers of the language being read and written. We'll now look briefly at the major themes and constructions that have guided L2 reading-writing connections research and instruction. Here we need to note from the start that L2 reading-writing scholars have been influenced heavily by the L1 perspectives we've just looked at. Indeed, these perspectives have served as the foundation from which much of the L2 research has been conducted. However, in accordance with the fact that L2 readers and writers are subject to some different influences than those affecting L1 readers and writers, we're going to see that L2 reading-writing scholarship has branched off in a number of new and intriguing directions.

As will be discussed a little later in this chapter, in the 1980s there was a fair amount of interest in the reading-writing connections field among L2 teachers and researchers. However, it wasn't until 1993, with the publication of Joan Carson and Ilona Leki's landmark book *Reading in the Composition Classroom: Second Language Perspectives,* that L2 reading-writing connections work was brought into a larger or more meaningful perspective. This collection of 18 papers provided a comprehensive view of approaches being taken to explore L2 reading-writing connections and the then current beliefs and findings about that field. Of greatest interest to us at the moment is the thematic approach taken in the book. After an introductory section that provided an overview of major themes and interests shaping the development of reading-writing connections as its own field of inquiry, Carson and Leki worked with two major themes:

- Cognitive perspectives
- Social perspectives

By structuring their book in this way, they made it clear that L2 teachers and researchers need an understanding of both the reading-writing processes at work *inside* students as they compose (the cognitive dimension) and the external/outside forces that must be accounted for in the development of L2 reading and writing abilities, such as the literacy-based demands of various academic discourse communities (social dimension). While asserting in their introduction that "reading and writing abilities are inextricably linked," they offered this description of changes taking place in the L2 writing field, which motivated the approach taken in their collection:

[From the early 1980s to the early 1990s] ESL writing classrooms have changed dramatically, focusing on writing as a communicative act and emphasizing students' writing processes and communicative intentions. Along with this change has come recognition of the extent to which reading can be, and in academic settings nearly always is, the basis for writing. Recent research has also called into question the traditional narrow view of the function of reading in the teaching of writing. (p. 1)

In this brief commentary, we gain a sense of why they chose to emphasize reading-writing connections from the perspective of reading playing a role in the writing classroom (as opposed to writing influencing reading instruction)—a critical move at a time when, as they point out, L2 writing teachers tended to assume that reading should be taught separately from writing and by reading teachers, not writing instructors. We also see, in their references to "communicative act" and "communicative intentions," why they chose to look at both the social and cognitive domains of L2 composing; that is, in line with the general trend in L2 language teaching to focus on the communicative purposes guiding students' language choices and expression and thus on the outer circumstances, such as audience, influencing communication, they acknowledged the need to look both inside and outside the L2 reader-writer. In their view, a true integration of reading and writing in the L2 writing classroom necessitated this dual cognitive and social emphasis.

Several years after Carson and Leki laid the foundations, Ferris and Hedgcock (1998) provided a revealing view of the range of themes and interests dominating L2 reading-writing instruction. They reviewed relevant literature in the following areas:

- Text as the source of literate knowledge
- Reading patterns in L1 and L2 literacy development
- Reading ability, writing proficiency, and interlingual transfer
- Reading-writing models: tools for teachers
- Social aspects of reading and writing in academic discourse communities
- English for academic purposes
- Reading and genre in academic writing

Although some of these themes overlap with theory and research in the L1 composing research, for the most part they signal a clear and strong branching off of L2 literacy research and practice from the L1 work that has played and continues to play an important role in preparing L2 reading-writing teachers and researchers to explore reading and writing from the L2 perspective.

They point out the value for L2 learners of exposure, through reading, to texts in the target language so as to build a knowledge base of the rhetorical and linguistic properties and operations of the L2. While reading performs the same function for acquisition of L1 literacy, its importance is enhanced in the L2 context, since students may lack the other kinds of language input readily available to native speakers of a language. Students in EFL contexts, for example, may have to rely heavily, if not exclusively, on what reading target language texts reveals to them about the L2, since opportunities for meaningful exposure to oral discourse may be limited or nonexistent. In these first two sections, then, we learn of the importance of teachers selecting appropriate texts and constructing meaningful reading experiences for L2 students so as to enrich overall target language acquisition as well as acquisition of L2 literacy knowledge and awareness.

The third theme they explore, which includes a focus on interlingual transfer, represents a major area of concentration in L2 literacy instruction and research. Here is where the L2 reading-writing connections field departs significantly from its L1 counterpart: as research has shown, L1 reading and writing skills can play an important role in the acquisition of L2 literacy skills (see, e.g., Carson, 1992; Carson, Carrell, Silberstein, Kroll, & Kuehn, 1990; Carson & Kuehn, 1992; Cumming, 1989; Cummins, 1979, 1980, 1984; Friedlander, 1990; Geva & Ryan, 1993; Hall, 1990; Kobayashi & Rinnert, 1992; Parry, 1996; Ringbom, 1992; Verhoeven, 1994; Whalen & Menard, 1995). Enabling learners to learn how to access and make effective use of their L1 literacy skills while reading and writing in the L2 is a key element in linking L2 reading and writing constructively.

The final three themes explored in Ferris and Hedgcock (1998) are also of value in conceptualizing L2 reading-writing instruction. In the first of these themes, focusing on academic discourse communities, the authors look at how "ESL composition teachers can play an important part in helping their students become members of any number of institutional and/or discipline-specific clubs or communities" (p. 37) by drawing their attention to the properties and conventions of reading and writing specific to various fields. Students interested in biology, for example, can be taught how biologists write for other biologists and how reading can be tied to this discipline-specific context. Because L2 writers are likely to lack knowledge of these disciplinary communities in terms of their reading-writing practices, enabling them to learn about these practices and thus guiding their entrance into these communities is now seen by many as a major goal of L2 writing instruction, at least at the college level. Here there is a strong link to the English for Academic Purposes (EAP) theme, in that the thrust of EAP instruction is to link teaching to the needs within specific contexts of L2 language use, including particular disciplinary communities. Within an EAP orientation, L2 writing teachers can concentrate on the specific characteristics of reading and writing in a particular context of academic use and can emphasize the learning of those characteristics in their classrooms. Likewise, researchers can study these various contexts of use and identify the ways in which reading and writing operate within them. The final theme covered—genre—is also a part of this picture, in that L2 writing teachers and researchers can focus on specific types of writing, such as critical review essays, and organize instructional practices around helping students understand and gain control of the features and principles of specific genres.

A more recent edited collection of L2 reading-writing scholarship, Belcher and Hirvela's (2001) *Linking Literacies: Perspectives on L2 Reading-Writing Connections,* draws on both traditional and emerging themes in the L2 reading-writing connections field. After an opening section consisting of papers that explore the research findings and theories that have formed the foundation of the reading-writing connections field, the editors organize the book around the following themes:

- In the classroom: teaching reading as writing and writing as reading
- (E)merging literacies and the challenge of textual ownership
- Technology-assisted reading and writing

The first of these sections revisits, from the L2 perspective, the themes explored as far back as Stotsky's (1983) review discussed earlier. This emphasis on the long-standing roles of reading and writing as supporting activities for each other reminds L2 writing teachers of the value of approaching L2 reading-writing instruction from this more traditional, yet still valuable, orientation. Meanwhile, the next two sections draw attention to newer ways of constructing L2 reading-writing relations. The section dealing with textual ownership and new literacies influenced by computer-mediated communication (CMC) draws together emerging research and beliefs concerning a complex aspect of L2 literacy that is attracting increasing interest: students' borrowing practices with respect to the use of source texts, as well as the closely related issue of plagiarism. With the advent of the Internet and students' access to virtually endless amounts of source texts via websites and other electronic databases, L2 writers now have at their disposal both an extraordinary resource for L2 reading and writing and a complicated new textual world in terms of what represents acceptable and unacceptable practices while using these new source texts. As will be discussed in Chapter 5, Internet-based reading and writing may now represent a primary contact point for L2 literacy learning and practice. Thus, as the relevant section in *Linking Literacies* demonstrates, L2 students' textual borrowing strategies and acts of what might be called plagiarism, via both traditional print texts and electronic texts, represent key new areas of L2 reading-writing connections research and practice. How students read these source texts and choose to incorporate, as writers, material from them into their written work is likely to be an especially important and interesting area of L2 reading-writing connections research and pedagogy. The same can be said of the final theme explored in *Linking Literacies:* the ways in which technology is affecting L2 reading and writing. Here, as in the previous section on textual borrowing and plagiarism, we see an emerging and important domain of interactions between reading and writing.

Grabe's extensive review of reading-writing literature in *Linking Literacies* also provides a valuable look at the themes and constructions central to the reading-writing connections field. Grabe's review stresses the need for understanding of these key theoretical/thematic domains:

- A theory of language
- A theory of learning

- A theory of language processing
- A theory of motivational and affective factors
- A theory of social-context influences
- A theory of background knowledge and its role in reading and writing

After a brief review of theories underlying the construction of these six major theoretical areas, Grabe explains:

> These theoretical positions, while in themselves neither theories of reading or writing, underlie any carefully thought-out view on reading and writing and their development. For example, to discuss reading, one must first understand how reading is processed, how language knowledge itself contributes, how background knowledge plays a role, how both social contexts and motivation influence abilities, and how learning is best accomplished for such goals. The same is true for writing abilities and for the contexts in which reading and writing interact. (pp. 17–18)

In his exploration of these theories and their links to reading-writing connections, he provides a valuable map for conceptualizing these connections. In a section called "Theories of Reading and Writing," for example, he stresses the need to study, separately, theories of reading and theories of writing in order to fully understand how the two skills support each other. He also provides a list of the processes writers must balance in their reading and writing (p. 21):

1. Planning for writing
2. Using language resources
3. Using background knowledge
4. Solving rhetorical problems
5. Reading to review text to that point
6. Balancing processes strategically
7. Monitoring outcomes
8. Revising plans and text appropriately

Later, in a section reviewing what he calls "new L1 research and new directions" relevant to theories of reading-writing relations, he identifies (p. 26) these areas as central to our continuing investigations of reading-writing connections:

1. Reading to write
2. Writing to read
3. Reading to learn and writing to learn
4. Reading multiple texts and writing outcomes

What is especially interesting here is that Grabe reiterates themes we've seen in earlier reviews of reading-writing connections. In other words, these core areas of reading-writing relationships remain at the heart of our work in linking reading and writing in research and classroom practice, albeit with an additional emphasis on themes explored in Belcher and Hirvela's volume, such as the role of technology in developing and utilizing reading-writing abilities. Thus, we can, in Grabe's view, continue to build our work in reading-writing connections on the ways in which these skills support each other (a point of view pursued in Chapters 3 and 4 of the present book).

Meanwhile, Grabe sees a particular need for research in these areas: L1/L2 literacy transfer; the role of "wide" or extensive reading in developing reading and writing knowledge; EAP; the "the roles of summarizing, using text models, note taking, and outlining, and using graphic organizers in reading and writing instruction" (p. 35); new approaches to curriculum development and their implications for reading-writing instruction (e.g., task-based and content-based instruction); and "the role of talk and discussion in the development of literacy abilities" (p. 36).

Additional Perspectives

Collectively, this review of major themes and perspectives concerning reading-writing connections shows that, while there is much that is new in this field (especially due to the growing role of technology in reading and writing), certain themes, such as the ways in which reading and writing *support* each other, cross the boundaries of history and the differences between L1 and L2 literacy. We've also seen continued expansion of the areas of interest related to reading-writing connections as we've moved from Stotsky's review in the early 1980s to those occurring more recently. Clearly, the field of reading-writing relations is dynamic in nature, with many challenges and opportunities ahead of us as teachers and/or researchers. As Grabe's review stresses, we need to understand the processes by which people learn to read and write a language, which includes how they learn the language itself and what skills and perspectives they bring or contribute to those processes (especially in the context of transferring L1 literacy skills to L2 literacy acquisition). We also need to look at reading and writing in the context of students working with multiple texts and text sources, including those that are electronically based. And we need to account for both the cognitive (internal) and social (external) aspects of reading and writing, including, in the case of the social, the conventions and demands of reading and writing within specific disciplinary communities.

At this point it's important to note that much of what we know about the ways in which reading and writing connect and about why it's so essential to look at the two skills in concert with each other comes from the study of these connections in the work of L1, or native English-speaking, writers. Much of that work will be addressed separately in upcoming chapters, but a brief and more global look at it at this point is helpful.

L1 researchers have focused heavily on a few key areas of research and practice: writing from sources (including summary writing and synthesizing, with a particular interest in writing from multiple source texts), writing-for-reading and reading-for-writing tasks, writing for learning (i.e., the use of writing in courses other than writing courses, such as in a history course, so as to gain deeper understanding of material read), and written response to literary texts. Tierney (1992) places the research in these areas in context by comparing beliefs and pedagogical practices in the 1970s and 1990s. Since these perspectives and the changes they reflect have played an important role in the development of ideas about L2 reading-writing connections, I show them in the two tables Tierney constructed (pp. 248–249).

In the first of these tables, he focused on *changes in viewpoints* about reading-writing relations:

1970s	1990s
Reading is receiving; writing is producing.	Reading and writing are composing, constructing, problem-solving activities.
Reading and writing are means of translating or transmitting ideas.	Reading and writing are vehicles for thinking.
Reading involves understanding the author's message; writing involves making your message clear for others.	Reading and writing involve interaction among participants as communicators, as well as the pursuit of self-discovery.
Reading and writing occur in a social context.	Reading and writing involve social processes.
Reading is a precursor to writing development.	Reading and writing development go hand in hand. Early writing is an avenue for reading development.
Writing development requires mastery of spelling conventions; reading development begins with mastery of skills and subskills.	Writing development involves invention as students pursue temporary spellings, negotiate conventions, etc. Reading development occurs naturally as students explore meaningful literacy experiences.

This comparison shows some significant changes in beliefs about reading and writing. By the 1990s, reading was being seen as an equal partner with writing in the co-construction of meaning, and this reflected a related belief in reading as something active, rather than passive, in nature. The shift to a view of reading and writing working together in pursuit of other aims—thinking, problem solving, and so forth—is also striking.

In his second table, Tierney shows how these shifting viewpoints were reflected in significant changes in classroom practice:

1970s	1990s
Reading and writing are taught separately.	Reading and writing are taught together.
Reading and writing skills are listed separately.	Reading and writing programs are developed from a list of skills and behaviors that apply to both processes.
Writing is excluded from reading; reading is excluded from writing.	Writing and reading occur together in collaboration.
Single texts are used to read or write.	Multiple texts are used to write, synthesize, pursue projects, develop reports, or analyze.
Beginning reading involves reading readiness activities.	Beginning reading involves shared reading and opportunities to write.
Early writing involves dictated stories and activities focused on mastering conventions.	Early writing involves allowing students to approximate and pursue conventions based on emerging hypotheses about language and how it works.

This comparison clearly reflects the impact of the changes in viewpoint described in the first table and represents a major shift in teaching practices. We see in the 1990s an emphasis on the idea that in teaching one skill, we are directly or indirectly teaching the other. Also note that the focus on reading and writing is based on multiple source texts as opposed to a single text—a shift toward intertextuality and a resulting need to use reading to help writing, and vice versa.

With this background in mind, we come to the important question, *from where do we draw our insights and perspectives on L2 reading-writing connections?* In addition to the L1 reading-writing literature, research in the field of **L1/L2 literacy transfer** is a rich source of knowledge and insight. Here, we want to know how and to what extent students are able to transfer their native language reading and writing skills and knowledge to their second language reading and writing activity. Much can also be learned from the field of **L2 reading.** Many of the contributions in this area rest in Krashen's (1984) oft-cited assertion that "it is reading that gives the writer the 'feel' for the look and texture" of written texts (p. 20). Many studies have focused on L2 readers' metacognitive knowledge or awareness of the features and operations of L2 texts and on how that knowledge shapes their own target language writing (e.g., Carrell, 1983, 1984, 1985, 1989, 1992; Carrell, Pharis, & Liberto, 1989; Carrell & Connor, 1991; Carrell & Eisterhold, 1983; Devine, 1993; Floyd & Carrell, 1987; Johnson, 1982; Li & Munby, 1996; Schoonen, Hultsjin, & Bossers, 1998). **Contrastive rhetoric,** with its investigations of differences across languages in terms of how material is organized and presented, is especially helpful with respect to providing insights into the kinds of reading-writing problems students may encounter as they make the transition from their L1 to the L2 (see, e.g., Connor, 1996; Connor & Kaplan, 1987; Panetta, 2001; Taylor & Taylor, 1995).

Studies of reading and writing tasks in various disciplines are also helpful because understanding reading-writing connections includes knowing about the kinds of reading-writing tasks students are expected to complete not just in English courses but also in other school subjects. Knowledge of these tasks allows L2 writing teachers to develop classroom tasks that prepare students for the connections between reading and writing expected in disciplines other than English. (Helpful sources here are Braine, 1995; Bridgeman & Carlson, 1984;

Carson, 2001; Carson, Chase, Gibson, & Hargrove, 1992; Casanave & Hubbard, 1992; Horowitz, 1986; Johns, 1981; Jenkins,
Jordan, & Weiland, 1993; Ostler, 1980; Pennington & Zhang,
1993; Spack, 1988.) The closely related fields of **English for
Specific Purposes** (ESP) and EAP are likewise valuable in this
regard.

Plagiarism, or students' unacceptable textual borrowing
practices, is an emerging source of important input as scholars examine how students process (as readers) source texts in
search of material to be incorporated into their own essays and
how they attempt (as writers) to achieve this inclusion of others' words and ideas. (See Barks & Watts, 2001; Bloch, 2001;
Deckert, 1993; Howard, 1993, 1995; Pecorari, 2001; Pennycook, 1994, 1996; Price, 2002; Scollon, 1994, 1995.) **Literacy
narratives** of reading and writing also generate important insights into L2 reading and writing. For instance, well-known
scholarship like Fan Shen's (1989) essay on his complex shifts
in rhetoric and identity (from reading and writing in his native Chinese to doing so in English) and collections of narratives like Helen Fox's (1994) *Listening to the World* and
Belcher and Connor's (2001) *Reflections on Multiliterate Lives*
provide rich, firsthand accounts of journeys through literacy
acquisition. Then there are case studies—that is, in-depth
qualitative investigations—of these same journeys. Some look
at K–12 immigrant students (e.g., Franklin, 1999; Hudelson,
1999; Macguire, 1999; Panferov, 2002), while others examine
college-level immigrants (e.g., Bosher, 1998; Harklau, 2000;
Hirvela, 1999a; Johns, 1992; Lam, 2000; Leki, 1999). Then there
are studies of undergraduate ESL students attending American
universities (e.g., Johns, 1991; Raimes, 1985, 1987; Smoke,
1994; Spack, 1997, and Zamel, 1983). Explorations of the L2
reading-writing encounters of graduate students have also
shed light on reading-writing connections issues (e.g., Angelova & Riazantseva, 1999; Arndt, 1987; Belcher, 1994;
Casanave, 1992, 1995; Connor & Kramer, 1995; Connor & Mayberry, 1996; Schneider & Fujishima, 1995).

A few words about the history of L2 reading-writing connections also help frame our initial understanding of these

connections. Matsuda's (2001) historical review essay focuses specifically on ESL and on the first 60 or so years of the 20th century. He looks at how the audiolingual movement, with its emphases on oral language over written language and on the teaching of grammatical structures through extensive drilling, prevented the development of independent interest in ESL composition—as well as any possible linking of reading and writing—until the early 1960s, when, as audiolingualism began to fall out of favor in language teaching circles, interest in written language began to grow. He also makes the important point that "the neglect of written language continues to be apparent in many aspects of L2 studies. In the field of second language acquisition, the amount of attention given to the acquisition of reading and writing competence is rather negligible" (p. 100). Kern and Warschauer (2000), in their treatment of the structural approach to language teaching as reflected in particular by audiolingualism, portray the modern historical context in this way:

> Approaches to the teaching of reading and writing also reflected the emphasis on structure. During the audiolingual period, reading was largely seen as an aid to the learning of correct structures; students were instructed to read out loud in order to practice correct pronunciation. Second-language writing instruction focused on students' production of formally correct sentences and paragraphs. At more advanced levels, contrastive rhetoric was used to provide examples of L1/L2 essay structure differences. In sum, the emphasis in speaking, reading, and writing was on the achieved linguistic product, not on cognitive or social processes. (p. 3)

Kern and Warschauer go on to briefly review the impact on reading-writing instruction of the cognitive and social or sociocognitive perspectives that gradually replaced or superseded structurally based approaches to language teaching. Of the cognitive emphasis that developed in the 1970s and dominated that era of reading and writing research, they explain:

The influence of cognitive approaches was seen quite strongly in the teaching of reading and writing. Following developments in first language reading and writing research, second language educators came to see literacy as an individual psycholinguistic process. Readers were taught a variety of cognitive strategies, both top-down (e.g., using schematic knowledge) and bottom-up (e.g., using individual word clues), in order to improve their reading process. Second language writing instruction shifted its emphasis from the mimicking of correct structure to the development of a cognitive, problem-solving approach, focused on heuristic exercises and collaborative tasks organized in staged processes such as idea generation, drafting, and revising. (p. 4)

With the shift in the 1980s to sociocognitive views of language learning that continue to exert a heavy influence on both L2 language and literacy instruction, they add, "reading and writing came to be viewed as processes embedded in particular sociocultural contexts" (p. 5). In both reading and writing instruction, students are taught to focus not only on their own individual reading and writing processes and strategies but on expectations for readers and writers in specific contexts of use; that is, within particular discourse communities, notions of what it means to read and write well will be tied to the practices and conventions common to those communities. Thus, in important domains of reading-writing instruction like EAP and ESP, teaching and learning are linked to the ways in which reading and writing are constructed within specific communities of use—for example, reading and writing as enacted in the business, legal, or scientific fields.

Reid's (1993a) historical account of L2 reading and writing looks at the ways in which reading and writing have been approached in four particular types of classrooms, arranged chronologically from the early 20th to late 20th century: grammar-translation classrooms, audiolingual classrooms, pattern-model classrooms, and process writing classrooms. Using as her unit of analysis the three key components of reading as related to writing—author, text, reader—she shows how the relationships between those components have changed, and she discusses the impact of these relationship shifts on the teaching of reading-writing connections. In the grammar-translation approach that dominated until around the 1940s, the emphasis in the classroom was on the author of an assigned text and the text itself; the student as reader/writer was not expected to negotiate or produce any meaning; instead, the student passively decoded the author's intended meaning in the assigned text. The reader/writer continued in that passive role in audiolingualism, Reid points out, though in this case most activity revolved around the assigned text itself. When teaching moved to the pattern-model pedagogy, students were asked to read sample texts that exemplified the writing patterns they were expected to adopt, and "teachers asked students to read, analyze, and then imitate the models" (Reid, 1993a, p. 37). What was especially significant here, Reid points out, is that students had to react to texts in the process of analyzing them and then had to incorporate input from them into their own writing. Thus, she says, there was a move "from the linear transmission models of reading, in which text information was said to be transferred directly to the passive, receptive reader, to an active model in which the reader participates by reacting to the text in the making of meaning" (p. 37). Here, then, the student as reader/writer had roughly equal status with the author of assigned reading material and the material itself, in that student input in reading and writing was now not only valued but encouraged. With the move in the 1980s to the process model of composition instruction that continues to dominate both the L1 and L2 writing fields, student response to reading material became a dominant aspect of the acts of reading and writing, as did an emphasis on ongoing composing (i.e., revisions of reading and writing and new constructions of meaning as students revisit the texts they read and write), leading to an emphasis on the idea that "meaning is created by the active negotiation between writer, text, and reader" (Reid, 1993a, p. 35). In this conceptualization, students use writing to unravel meaning in texts being read and use input from reading to shape what is being written.

With respect to historical conditions, then, we see that interest in L2 reading-writing connections is a fairly recent development and that it has occurred at least in part as notions of language learning and teaching have changed from a structural to a communicative orientation. And, as we saw earlier, several domains of research have emerged as particularly important sources of insight into relationships between reading and writing in second language contexts.

Conclusion

In this opening chapter, we've looked at some of the ways in which reading-writing connections have been conceptualized or presented and at some primary sources of input for increased understanding of those connections. We've also seen, in the tables provided by Tierney, an overview of changes that have taken place with regard to how reading and writing are treated in composition instruction. What we have not seen is a comprehensive or definitive model of L2 reading-writing connections from which to base our continued investigations, in research and practice, of such connections. At this point, there is no such model. As Grabe (2001) suggests in his extensive literature review cited earlier, this model building is problematic because a true model of this type must account, simultaneously, for the inclusion of reading in a theory of writing instruction and a theory of writing in reading instruction. In domains such as writing to read (discussed in Chapter 3 in the present book) and reading to write (discussed in Chapter 4), much is known about how to guide instruction in each of these directions, that is, with writing used to support reading and reading used to support writing. However, building a model that binds these two themes or directions into one unified whole is an elusive business, particularly when we must take into account, in the L2 field, the characteristics that separate it from the L1 field. In L2, for example, we're dealing with language learners striving to achieve a multitude of competencies in a language and a rhetoric not their own. We're also dealing with whatever influences might be exerted by their native language literacy skills and aware-ness and the complex L1–L2 transfer issues that come into play. What's more, there are wide-ranging learning styles and strategies to contend with. Imagine, then, a classroom at the elementary, high school, or college level comprised of stu-dents from several different linguistic, rhetorical, and cultural backgrounds possessing varying degrees of L1 literacy. What must be done to build a model of L2 reading-writing connec-tions that can comfortably accommodate these variables?

While we cannot at this point cite a complete model of L2 reading-writing connections, we can draw from ideas and findings presented in the L1 literature and from the sources of input discussed earlier. We can also work with a set of be-liefs about reading-writing relations that has emerged over the past few decades. In addition to accepting Hunt's (1985) an-ecdotal observation that "common sense dictates that reading and writing are related" (p. 159), we can base our research and practice on the core notion that "reading and writing are as inseparable as two sides of the same coin" (Peritz, 1993, p. 382), a belief that is at the heart of the work discussed in the remainder of this book. And, as teachers of writing, we can take to heart Bartholomae and Petrosky's (1987) oft-cited as-sertion that "there is no better place to work on reading than in a writing course" (p. iii), as well as Spack's (1988) belief, arising from the reading-writing research, that "to become bet-ter writers . . . students need to become better readers" (p. 42). Finally, as a starting point in our construction of the L2 writ-ing class as a site for linking reading and writing, we can em-brace Lunsford's (1978) frequently quoted claim (with refer-ence to L1 writing teachers) that "the teacher of writing must automatically and always be a teacher of reading as well" (p. 49). Words like *automatically* and *always* in this statement may seem extreme and indeed may not be appropriate in many L2 writing instruction scenarios, given that we, unlike L1 writing teachers, are working with learners of a new language, a new rhetoric, and a new culture. However, the underlying tenor of Lunsford's statement—that it is important for writing for the writing teacher to see her or himself as a teacher of reading in addition to writing—establishes a baseline principle that the rest of this book operates from.

With respect to where the L2 reading-writing field now stands in its understanding and practice, the situation is perhaps best described by Grabe's (2001) statement that "one of the most consistent implications of two decades of research on reading and writing relations is that they should be taught together and that the combination of both literacy skills enhances learning in all areas" (p. 25). Then we have the "socioliterate" pedagogy outlined most prominently in the work of Johns (1997)—a pedagogy that, she explains, accounts for the "texts, roles, and contexts" that students encounter in their attempts to acquire L2 academic literacy. This emphasis on the socioliterate pedagogy brings into play, as well, ideas about critical theory or practice and locating academic literacy acquisition in larger social contexts, as articulated by, among others, Benesch (2001); Kutz, Groden, and Zamel (1993); and Rodby (1992). Bearing all these perspectives in mind, here are a few beliefs or principles that have emerged as L2 reading-writing connections as a field of its own has gradually developed.

- Writing teachers need to be aware of theories of L2 reading and to associate those with, not separate them from, theories of writing.
- Reading provides a vital source of linguistic and rhetorical input for writing, so that writing assignments should be seen to start in acts of reading and to be sustained and informed by acts of reading, rather than to follow such acts.
- Reading, like writing, is an act of composing (not decoding), so that, when we teach writing skills, we have occasions for teaching reading as well.
- Writing assignments involving reading and writing about more than one source text provide richer con-

texts for linking the acts of reading and writing than do those involving a single source text.

- Literature (especially fictional texts) is a valuable resource for bringing reading and writing together.
- Writing and reading tasks are more meaningful for students—and more natural sites for connecting reading and writing—when they're linked to the tasks students perform in other settings, such as other courses or out-of-school locations.
- Students should be given opportunities to *talk* about their encounters with reading and writing.
- Reading and writing need to be presented as recursive in nature, that is, as activities involving back-and-forth movement between them, as it is this kind of movement that helps link them.

These operating principles will be seen in greater detail in the remaining chapters of this book, and through the elaboration and illustration of them, we'll see a picture of the L2 writing teacher very different from the picture that dominated prior to the 1980s. This will be a picture of a writing teacher who thinks of writing *as* reading and reading *as* writing and who looks for opportunities to help students break through their common preoccupation with these skills as separate entities. It seems likely that, for many students working in their L2, writing and reading are assumed to occur apart from each other ("First I'll do my reading for the assignment, and later I'll write my essay"), so that what each skill can contribute to the other is not recognized. Then there is the likelihood that when students encounter problems in one domain, they may fail to understand that the genesis of the problems may rest in the other skill—for example, that problems in writing may actually start in problems with reading. If students' acquisition of meaningful, effective academic literacy is our goal as L2 writing teachers, we must conduct our classes as places where the two anchors of literacy—reading and writing—are both accounted for in significant ways. This presupposes that we construct the L2 writing classroom as a place where *literacy,* not strictly writing skill, is the real focus of the course; where we believe that to learn about writing without learning about reading—and how reading contributes to writing—is to deprive our students of a true *composing* experience that is at the heart of writing.

Questions for Reflection and Discussion

1. Based on your own experience, does the core notion of "reading as an act of composing" seem acceptable? Why or why not?
2. The focus of this chapter has been on the reading and writing of English. What about other languages? In your L1 (if it isn't English) or your L2 (if English is your L1), do the ideas reviewed in this chapter apply? If not, why not? If so, to what extent?
3. What's your response to the Andrea Lunsford quote on p. 37: "The teacher of writing must automatically and always be a teacher of reading as well"? To what extent do you agree or disagree with her assertion? Why?
4. It was pointed out in this chapter that there is, as yet, no complete model of L2 reading-writing connections. How important is it to construct such a model?
5. A point posited throughout this chapter (and this book) is that reading needs to be incorporated into the writing classroom, but what has not been made clear is what proportion of a writing course the reading component should occupy. What recommendation would you make for the proportioning of reading and writing? For example, equal treatment of the two skills, or 75 percent writing and 25 percent reading, or a 60-40 split? On what basis should such a decision be made?

6. What, at this point in time, is your own philosophy with respect to reading-writing connections (L1 or L2)? If you had to state your philosophy in one sentence, what would it be?

Chapter 2
Linking Reading and Writing through Reader-Response Theory

In Chapter 1 we reviewed the major perspectives underlying the core notion of reading and writing as connected to each other in various ways. Collectively, these perspectives characterize both reading and writing as productive, meaning-making activities utilizing many of the same composing skills, during a process in which reading informs writing and writing informs reading. Now that we've seen these perspectives, we can begin examining reading-writing connections not only as they occur in theory and research but as they can be enacted in classroom practice.

In this chapter we look primarily at the *reading* side of the notion of reading-writing connections. Here it is interesting to note that the key phrase *reading-writing connections* (the phrase nearly always used in the professional literature) begins with *reading,* not *writing.* That's mainly because in classroom settings where students are reading and writing, their first acts of composing generally occur as *readers* as they engage the assigned reading materials (newspaper or magazine articles, stories, poems, textbooks, scholarly articles or books, web-based documents, etc.). Furthermore, the centrality of reading is maintained throughout the writing process because (a) students frequently consult, through reading, the text(s) they are writing about as they search for information, quotations, or other material to include in their writing; and (b) they read and reread their own writing as they compose the text they are writing. As we can see, then, reading takes place almost continually in classroom reading-writing situations, and so it is vital for us as teachers to understand our students as *readers*. Knowing them as readers helps us understand and work with them as writers.

For many teachers, such common reading-writing connections statements as "good writers are good readers" and "good readers are good writers" may seem obvious and therefore easy to apply in classroom practice. In truth, however, linking reading and writing effectively in the classroom can be problematic. For example, non-native-speaking (NNS) students at the high school and college levels bring with them a background as writers and readers in their native language. They have been taught and have formed notions of reading and writing as defined by the ways in which speakers of their native language read and write—ways that may well differ from reading and writing in English (or whatever target language the students are studying), as the field of contrastive rhetoric has demonstrated. While these established L1 literacy practices can and often do impact positively on students' L2 reading and writing, they can also interfere with how students view and approach writing and reading in the L2. Then, too, the teacher might find it difficult to measure or interpret the influence of the student's L1 literacy skills and knowledge.

Suppose, for instance, that a high school ESL teacher suddenly finds herself teaching a newly arrived student from, say, Vietnam. What if she is not familiar with reading and writing in Vietnamese? How much can she reasonably be expected to know about her student's Vietnamese literacy skills? Furthermore, many writing teachers (1) may not regard themselves as reading teachers or feel qualified to teach reading and (2) may not be sufficiently familiar with theories and models of reading to factor reading into their writing instruction. In addition to defining themselves as *writing* teachers, they may know or think of their students primarily, if not exclusively, as writers. After all, as writers they supply teachers with a concrete product—a book report, an essay, a summary, and so forth—that can be assessed by the various criteria we use when evaluating writing. What cannot be measured clearly or easily is the reading students did in preparation for the writing. How did they read the assigned material? How did they conceptualize the act of reading in the L2? What reading problems occurred? How much did those problems impact on their writing? To what extent did their L1 literacy background help or hinder their reading (and thus their writing) in the assignment? Administering tests of reading comprehension will not necessarily tell us about the world of reading our students inhabit and the ways in which they construct reading, particularly when we're looking at reading as it applies to writing. We need to do much more than administer such tests if we are to bring L2 reading and writing together for our students, especially if we lack specialized knowledge of or training in reading theory and instruction.

In this chapter we work with the idea that we need to know as much about students' performance and experiences as readers as we know about their involvement as writers, particularly since, as we saw in Chapter 1, the composing processes at work in reading and writing overlap. To make the "'reading-writing connection" work successfully in our classes, we need a clear understanding of students as readers: their notions of reading (especially "good reading"), how they were taught to read their native language and/or the L2, their approaches to reading, their problems and fears as readers, and so forth. This, in turn, requires that we sometimes foreground students' activity as readers in the process of teaching writing. Instead of following the traditional practice of treating reading as a passive activity that operates separately from writing, we must view reading as an integral part of the writing process and establish a window through which to more closely observe the joint composing processes underlying our students' reading and writing. To do so requires a mechanism that enables us to enter into the world of our students' reading, the world that underscores and shapes their writing and that in turn is influenced and informed by their writing experiences.

This chapter explores an area of theory and practice that has shed considerable light on readers and reading: **reader-response theory.** At the elementary school and high school levels in particular, reader-response theory has heavily influenced the design of L1 language arts and English courses through the work of such well-known teachers/scholars as Louise Rosenblatt, Judith Langer, Alan Purves, Richard Beach, and Robert Probst. The focus here will be on reader-response theory because it offers teachers and researchers invaluable opportunities to penetrate into the domain of reading that both precedes and intertwines with writing in contexts where students write from and about texts they have read. We'll examine how this collection of theories has reconstructed views of readers and reading in ways that enrich the teaching of writing and draw close attention to the composing processes at the heart of reading-writing relationships. After reviewing the major concepts and components of reader-response theory, we'll explore some practical applications of reader-response theory in writing instruction at the high school and college level.

Reader-Response Theory: A Definition

Reading is considered to involve three main elements: *the author of a text, the text itself, and the reader of the text.* For a long time the main interest was in the authors of texts and what they intended when they wrote their texts. For example, what were Dickens' purposes in *Great Expectations?* What did he want readers to take away from that novel? Traditionally, readers were expected to determine what an author's purposes were, and good readers were those who could make such determinations with a high degree of accuracy. Reading instruction thus meant training readers to track down an author's intentions and then react to the text in the context of what the author was attempting to do. Then, in the 20th century, the emphasis shifted to the texts themselves, with little or no interest in the author's history or intentions. In this "new critical" or "formalist" approach, meaning existed in the text alone, and the reader's job was to locate that meaning through analysis of the text's structure and language.

Reader-response theory takes a significantly different approach to reading. It says that the *reader* is, if not the most important figure in this author/text/reader combination (as many reader-response theorists would maintain), at least an equal partner in a dialogue among these three parties. Therefore, we can define reader-response theory as an approach to reading that primarily examines and values *readers* and how readers read texts, not how or why authors wrote them or how they are organized. As Richard Beach (1993) explains, in reader-response theory the concern is with "how readers make meaning from their experience with the text" (p. 1). That, in fact, is the key element in a definition of reader-response theory: the reader's *experience* while traveling through a text.

Reader-Response Theory: Background

The roots of reader-response theory are in the field of literary theory and are generally seen to originate in the work of the influential British literature and reading specialist I. A. Richards. While teaching literature courses at Cambridge University in the 1920s, Richards was struck by problems his students had when interpreting English poetry. To better understand their responses, Richards instructed the students to write "protocols"—that is, explications of poems that described, in part, how and why the students interpreted them as they did. To minimize the influence of forces outside the poems themselves and thus create more space in which to examine the students' responses and response processes, Richards withheld from the students the names of and any information about the authors of the poems. His analysis of the protocols focused on what motivated the students' interpretations, and in the process, it shifted interest to the "aesthetics of response" (Freund, 1987). This was a stark contrast to the aforementioned traditional emphasis of literary theory on the *authors* of literary texts and the personal and historical factors influencing what and how they produced their texts.

Richards shifted attention from the author—and to some extent from the text—to the reader. His classic work of literary theory, *Practical Criticism* (1929), described and analyzed the results of his protocol experiments and initiated what eventually became a deep interest among literary theorists in the reader and in reading processes, reflected most dramatically (though not exclusively) in Roland Barthes' well-known declaration of the "birth of the reader" and the "death of the author" (1989) and in Stanley Fish's much debated question "Is there a text in this class?" (1980). Richards altered the course of literary theory and paved the way toward important new understandings of reading, because, says Fowler (1971), he "located the complexity [of a commentary on a text] in the reader's responses rather than in the linguistic structure of texts" (p. 109). Current reading theory and research relies to some extent on the reader-based approach introduced by Richards as a means of better understanding how students compose readings.

Because it is primarily associated with the field of literary theory, reader-response theory may initially seem misplaced in discussions of writing instruction, particularly L2 writing instruction. However, Newkirk (1986) has pointed out that "reader-response theory has stirred interest in the moment-by-moment process of reading, an interest that parallels work in the writing process" (p. 5). White (1994) notes that reader-response theory "brings reading and writing together as parallel acts, both consisting of the making of meaning: The writer seeks to make meaning of experience, while the reader seeks to make meaning out of a text" (p. 97).

By placing the reader at the center of its inquiries, reader-response theory has made possible important insights into how readers read, has provided a means by which such inquiries can be conducted, and has brought into closer focus similarities between the reading and writing processes. Furthermore, it has broken what might be called the traditional hegemony or control of the text and the writer. Many writing teachers who assign writing tasks based on reading and source texts may see only the meaning *they* believe is embedded in the texts based on their own reading. They may also expect or require that their students will read those texts exactly as they have. Or they may insist that students embark on a quest to determine the *author's* intended meaning or theme(s). What may be lost in the equation is how *students* approach and interpret the assigned texts as readers and how the means by which they compose their readings will influence the reading itself as well as the writing that follows. Some teachers may assume that students need only passively locate relevant meaning already situated in the text and simply extract that meaning to serve the writing purpose at hand. Reader-response theory challenges that view, says Stubbs (1986), by asserting that "the meaning of a text does not just sit 'in' the text waiting to be taken out by readers, but . . . readers actively construct the meaning in light of their background interests and expectations" (p. 117); that is, reader-response theory acknowledges and investigates the influences students bring to the act of reading, influences that will indirectly or directly impact on their writing, in part because of the ways in which they have shaped the reading on which their writing is based. This is an especially important emphasis in the L2 context, where students carry into their reading and writing ideas about and approaches (to reading and writing) that are shaped by their L1 rhetorical and cultural backgrounds. Instead of being neutral, passive readers and writers, they function in a rich and complex social context in which they may rely on a host of previously formed or taught L1 beliefs and practices concerning literacy and culture as well as those associated with their L2, as social constructivist theories of writing assert. Reader-response theory corresponds closely with these social theories and, in the process, becomes a valuable tool in writing instruction by creating a theoretical foundation from which students can, through writing, explore the influences that construct or shape their reading processes.

A central belief in reader-response theory, is that "a text is not a puzzle or a dictator; it is a partner in a dialogue, in a negotiation" (Leki, 1993, p. 21). The other partner is, of course, the reader, and the dialogue is, as White (1994) explains, "a creative interaction between reader and text" (p. 91). In the writing classroom, that reader is also a writer, and the negotiation, or dialogue, between her and the assigned text involves composing processes common to both reading and writing. By invoking the image of a dialogue, then, reader-response theory contributes to reading and writing instruction and investigations of reading-writing connections by highlighting the meaning-making and interactive nature of the acts of reading and writing. In even the simplest of dialogues—say, two people discussing the price of strawberries—there is a contribution from each partner in the dialogue as they exchange comments. By positioning the reader as contributing to a dialogue between reader, text, and author, reader-response theory posits a connection between reading and writing when writing is used in relationship to what has been read.

While there are in fact several theories comprising the collective term *reader-response theory,* what they have in common is that "most of them begin by asking questions about the reader's experience in the act of reading the text" (Selden, 1989, p. 10). Based on the constructs of reader-response theory, "we can no longer talk about the meaning of a text without considering the reader's contribution to it" (Selden, 1989, p. 132). Culler (1982) makes a similar point: "To speak of the meaning of the work is to tell a story of reading. . . . The structure and meaning of a work emerge through an account of the reader's activity" (p. 35). These perspectives are vital in any writing classroom where our students are expected to read texts and then write using those texts in some way. What and how our students write is closely related to how they have read the assigned texts. Poor reading of texts is likely to result in poor writing about them, in which case we cannot simply regard a student's weak essay as the by-product of problems in writing. We need to understand the student's problems or limitations in *reading,* because the act of writing about the texts began with the reading of them. Hence, we need to equip our students to be effective readers of the texts we assign or that they read in other courses, and this necessitates understanding reading and its relation to writing as well as the ways in which students perform as readers. This is where reader-response theory contributes to and enriches our understanding of connections between reading and writing. By privileging the reader and the act of reading (rather than the text) through a reader-oriented approach, we are better able to explore students' composing processes, processes that, as we have already seen, are frequently the same in writing as they are in reading. Adopting a reader-response view of reading and writing allows us to examine students' experiences as readers and unravel the "story of reading" Culler (1982) refers to.

In a reader-response framework, rather than assuming that students begin to write after they have read the assigned texts, we assume that they have already composed a text (or a set of texts, if they are reading more than one) before the physical act of writing begins. Furthermore, we assume that at least to some degree, this new text that they have composed will be reflected in what they write. The writing that follows reflects the composing during reading that has already taken place and that therefore will influence the act of writing. In order to ensure that the writing that students eventually produce is effective and to better understand problems students have encountered in their writing, we need to trace that writing back to its source: students' composing activity as readers. Reader-response theory provides the philosophical foundation, the theoretical framework, and the tools by which we can operate, as writing teachers, in this way.

Reader-Response Theory: Components

Privileging the reader in the way reader-response theory does is not an indication that the text or the author's intentions are irrelevant or of little importance when discussing student reading of a text. While some reader-response theorists embrace the notion of the "death of the author" and feel that all meaning resides in the reader, many take a middle-ground approach, as reflected in Leki's use of the "dialogue" and "negotiation" images (cited in the preceding section). Culler (1980) explains that "in concentrating on the reader one is not attempting to strip the author of all his glory, suggesting that he does nothing and that the reader does all; one is simply recognizing that the activities of readers provide more and better evidence about the conditions of meaning" (p. 51).

This point of view has been articulated most prominently by Louise Rosenblatt, whose pioneering book *Literature as Exploration* (1938/1976) was the first attempt to link reader-oriented theories to the English writing classroom. Rosenblatt's work proposed what she calls the *transactional* view of reading, one that essentially places the text and the reader on equal footing: "The reader's main purpose is to participate as fully as possible in the potentialities of the text" (1978, p. 69). The outcome of the reading of a text is a combination of the text's/author's intentions and the reader's own intentions and influences while reading. Probst (1990) elaborates on this when he says that "the reader performs *with* the text" (p. 29). In the transaction that occurs between text and reader, a new text is created, one jointly influenced by the original text and the reader's activity while reading the text. It is that newly created text that we as teachers need to understand and that we can draw to our students' attention through a reader-response focus in our instruction.

The images used in reader-response descriptions of texts and the acts of reading them also contribute to the value reader-response theory holds for the linking of reading and writing. For example, "texts . . . are plural, open to a number of interpretations. Meanings are not fixed or given, but are released in the process of reading" (Belsey, 1980, pp. 19–20). Eco (1984) distinguishes between "open" and "closed" texts as a way of showing how different kinds of texts allow for a greater or lesser degree of reader-text transactions. For instance, literary texts are open to a wide range of interpretations, while an objective explanation of a theory or a process in, say, a textbook for an introductory course in biology is, by intention, closed to any interpretive action on the part of the reader. Electronically based hypertexts, in which readers are free to make their own links while negotiating the document, are a new form of "open" text, one many of our students will be engaging in 21st-century literacy practice. The influential reader-response theorist Wolfgang Iser speaks of texts having "blanks," "gaps," "vacant spaces," and "horizons of possibilities" (1974, 1978), all of which the reader fills in conjunction with the directions suggested by the text. In Iser's view (1974), the reader's "reactions are not set out for him, but he is simply offered a frame of possible decisions, and when he has made his choice, then he will fill in the picture accordingly" (p. 55). Reading, Iser adds, is a "process of anticipation and retrospection" on the part of the reader as she or he works through the text (p. 290). As the reader fills in "blanks" and "vacant spaces," earlier theories about the meaning of the text are reexamined and rejected or refined in light of the additional perspective gained by the ongoing gap-filling activity. This reader-oriented view of reading coincides with Frank Smith's (1971) groundbreaking conceptualization of reading as a process of "hypothesis testing" and with Kenneth Goodman's (1968) portrait of reading as a "psycholinguistic guessing game" in which readers revise their expectations for and interpretations of texts as they learn more about the texts while reading them. While reading recursively—that is, moving forward and backward through the text—readers reject earlier hypotheses about the text and create new ones to reflect their added insight into the text, or, more accurately, the new text they compose as they encounter and reencounter the original text. In other words, they *compose* a reading in much the same way that writers compose the text they write, that is, through a combination of false starts, of revisions based on rereading of the earlier attempts to write the text, and of constructing new ideas about the shape the text will take while writing and evaluating it. Reader-response theory, then, operates with images and concepts of composing processes in reading (e.g., Iser's "horizons of possibilities") that correspond to those at work in writing and writing instruction.

Advantages of Reader-Response Theory

Reader-response theory serves as a valuable tool for privileging and investigating students' composing processes as readers, processes that can both influence and overlap with their composing processes as writers. Given the complexities of reading and writing in a second or foreign language, the need for a means by which reading and writing processes can be foregrounded in planning for teaching and in individual work with students is considerable. While reader-response theory is not the only construct by which these processes can receive proper attention in instruction, it may be especially well suited to L2 writing instruction involving reading and writing, because students themselves may not see a connection between the acts of reading and writing and might perform one act in isolation from the other, even when they are reading a source text for a writing assignment. In their prior experiences in English classes, for example, reading and writing may have been taught as separate skills. Adopting a reader-oriented approach enables a teacher to show students critical relationships between reading and writing through a focus on students' composing processes. Furthermore, for students who feel insecure about themselves as L2 readers, the reader-response approach empowers them by showing them that they, not the text (or not the text alone), are at the center of reading. It tells them that they have a legitimate, meaning-making role to play while reading. It also allows them to examine how their L1 reading strategies may be influencing their L2 reading and perhaps interfering with (or assisting) the writing that follows.

Reader-response theory is also valuable in the context of reading-writing relations because, as noted briefly earlier, its principles coincide with those operating in the social constructivist view that has heavily influenced L2 writing instruction in recent years. Both reader-response theory and social constructivist views argue that students do not act on

neutral ground when they read and write a text in the L2. Social theories argue, instead, that our students bring to the act
of L2 reading and writing ideas about and definitions of literacy already acquired and practiced in their learning of literacy skills in their native language—that is, what Eskey (1993)
refers to as the "sociolinguistics of literacy" (p. 227). Or, "the
meaning of a text depends on who is reading it" (Leki, 1993,
p. 21). By the same token, an essay written by a student depends on who has written it, including how she or he read the
source texts linked to the assignment, how she or he related
the texts to the requirements of the assignment, and how she
or he defined the nature of the assignment. For instance, a student's notion of an "argument" essay may differ considerably
from what the teacher giving the assignment has in mind, depending on the student's native culture and L1 rhetoric and
on how the notion of argument or persuasion is constructed
in that framework.

Ferris and Hedgcock (1998) urge writing teachers to remember that "literacy acquisition never occurs in a vacuum"
(p. 36). This point refers not only to the L1 influences students
may bring to L2 reading and writing but also to the purposes
for and contexts in which they may perform their L2 reading
and writing. As has been shown most notably in work by
Swales (1990) and other genre analysts, students at higher levels of academic writing instruction belong to specific discourse communities possessing their own conventions or expectations for reading and writing (such as a field like biology)
and may be required to produce certain genres or types of
writing within these conventions (such as a research-based
paper). ESL students in high schools will likewise face expectations for their reading and writing, in the increasingly
widespread proficiency exams they are required to pass in order to graduate. In all of these situations, students' ideas about
reading and writing have been socially constructed; that is,
they have been shaped by the needs and definitions pertain-
ing to specific literacy situations at hand as well as by students' own L1-based ideas about reading and writing.

We now need to conceive of writing "as a social exchange

within the classroom," says Beach (1993, p. 111), and this necessitates adopting an approach to writing instruction that accounts for notions of reading and writing that students carry
into the classroom as well as for the situations in which they
will need to read and write in the L2. This will be especially
important where students are engaged in writing related to
reading, because both the reading and writing practices of the
students will be socially constructed, rather than neutral activities devoid of influences and expectations. Using a reader-
response approach as our basis for teaching writing, we can
create room in which to examine the socially based composing processes of our students and so learn to better understand
why they read and write as they do. This understanding can
lead us to writing instruction that touches directly on the
problems and concerns our students experience.

The reader-response approach opens teachers' and students' eyes to the composing processes at the heart of reading
and writing, because it acknowledges and values the diversity
of these approaches found among students. Like social constructivist views, reader-response theory helps a teacher to
recognize that a class composed of 25 students consists of
25 separate (though perhaps closely related) sets of composing processes (not one set duplicated 25 times), and it creates
avenues by which those processes can be explored and understood.

Two Classroom-Based Reader-Response Scenarios

Now let's examine how reader-response theory can be applied
in the classroom and what is to be gained in terms of teaching and learning. We first explore a common high school English assignment—one that an ESL student placed into a
mainstream English class is likely to face—and look at what
an ESL teacher using a similar assignment could gain by employing a reader-response approach to the assignment. Then
we'll follow the same procedure at the college level.

A High School Scenario

The teaching of English in American high schools, public and private, is dominated by an emphasis on literature, both literature for its own sake and literature as a tool in the teaching of writing, especially within a response-centered mode in which students develop their writing skills through responses to literary texts (Applebee, 1992). As many of us know, "The formal essay about literature is one of the standard features of life in many English classrooms" (Beach and Marshall 1991, p. 91). This type of essay, in which students are expected to construct an interesting and carefully developed response to the assigned text, is a perfect example of reading-writing connections at work, in that students compose both a reading of the literary text (which, by its imaginative nature, invites reader reconstruction of the text) and their writing about it. Likewise, how they read the text will impact heavily on what and how they write about it. For ESL students at the high school level, this may prove to be a daunting task, especially because of the often elusive nature of the term *response.* What does it actually mean to "respond" to something? To some students, a summary is a form of response; to others, responding means to express an opinion about a text. How can we, as teachers, prepare L2 students to perform a response-based task? Let's look at a reader-response approach to the reading side of this situation.

One of the literary works frequently assigned in American high school English classes is J. D. Salinger's famous and controversial novel *The Catcher in the Rye,* about a teenage boy, Holden Caulfield, who suffers an emotional breakdown when he is unable to cope with what he sees as the hypocrisy of the adult world. His rebellious nature and intriguing insights into human behavior have made him a compelling figure, if not a hero, to countless young people since the novel was published in 1951. For a recently arrived ESL student, however, there may be numerous difficulties in understanding the character of Holden Caulfield, the conditions he reacts against, and the ways in which he rebels, rendering (for many students) the reading of the novel a complex task at best and a nightmare at worst. If so, the challenge of writing the assigned response essay will be enormous to many of our students, since the writing is an outgrowth of the reading. Struggles in reading the novel almost inevitably will result in problems writing the assigned response essay. Therefore, we need to find ways to help our students in their reading, and that means developing an understanding of how they approach it.

We can use a reader-response approach to this scenario in two primary ways—pre-reading and post-reading exercises. In each case, we will focus on students' experience with the text.

In the pre-reading phase, we will ask them to explore, verbally and/or in writing, a series of questions designed to lead them into a positive reading experience with the text. In addition to providing valuable information (to both students and teachers) about the students as readers, these questions direct students' attention away from deep concerns about the complexity of the text and the author's intentions—concerns that might act as barriers to students' reading of the text. Such concerns (which are entirely understandable for the L2 reader, who may be making her or his first attempt at reading a literary work in English) can be barriers in the sense that they can lead to unnecessary anxiety or fear over baseline comprehension of the text and cause students to get bogged down in bottom-up reading aimed at decoding the text word by word and sentence by sentence. The reader who is caught up in such worries may be unable to enjoy or appreciate the experience of engaging the story being told. Furthermore, these worries can cause L2 readers to cast themselves in the limited role of passive participants whose sole responsibility in reading is locating meanings embedded in the text. Students who are addressing response-based pre-reading questions will be encouraged to see themselves as active meaning-makers contributing to their reading. In this way, reading moves out of the receptive role it has often been characterized as occupying in the traditional language teaching breakdown where writing and speaking are productive and reading and listening are the passive or receptive skills. Communicating this view of reading and readers to students is one of the primary goals of reader-response theory when applied to classroom practice.

Using reader-response theory as our instructional basis, here are some of the pre-reading questions we might ask students to address (ideally in writing, but also verbally, in classroom discussion) *before* they begin reading *A Catcher in the Rye:*

1. What strategies or approaches do you use when you read a novel (or other text types)? For example, do you first gather information about the author or the historical period in which the text was written? Do you take notes while you read the text? [This question could be used regardless of the reading assignment.]

2. What strategies or approaches do you plan to use when you read *The Catcher in the Rye?* Have you formed any ideas as to how you plan to read the novel? Do you think you will read the novel the same way you would a novel in your native language?

3. What are your feelings about reading a novel in English? Have you read any novels prior to *The Catcher in the Rye?* Do you feel confident or uncertain as you enter this reading experience? If you feel some uncertainty, what, specifically, are you concerned about? What kinds of problems, if any, do you expect to have?

4. When you encounter problems with vocabulary or confusing information in a text, how do you usually try to solve those problems? What will you do if this happens while reading *The Catcher in the Rye?*

5. After you read *The Catcher in the Rye,* you will have to write a *response essay* about it. At this point, what does the phrase *response essay* mean to you? Also, while you read the novel, will you think about

the essay you will have to write later? Will you try to keep track of your responses while you read (e.g., by taking notes about, say, your responses to the main character, Holden Caulfield, after each chapter of the novel)? What do you think are effective ways to help prepare yourself to write the response essay?

6. What is your interpretation, at this point, of the novel's title, *The Catcher in the Rye?* If you feel you don't know what the title means, will this have any effect on your confidence or approach while reading the novel? In your opinion, how important is it to understand a book's title before you read it?

7. How important is it, in your view, to try to understand the author's intentions while reading a novel? What about other text types? In this assignment you will be asked to look only for what you think the book is about, not for what you believe the author wants you to think. Are you comfortable with this approach to reading? Will it be more difficult or easier to read with this focus on yourself, not the author?

Note that in these questions, the focus is not on the text itself or the author, other than in a minor way in Question 6 and a little more in Question 7—and even there the real concentration is on the reader, not the title. Instead, and in accordance with reader-response theory, the focus is on the student as *reader.* Whereas a traditional classroom approach might be to ask students to gather information about the author or the historical period in which a book was written, the teacher has indirectly told the students that her/his interest is in *them,* not the text or the author. Note how often the words *you* and *what do you think* are used in these questions. Furthermore, the answers teachers receive will enable them to address, in advance of the reading of the novel, any problems they anticipate for the students based on their responses. As teachers we are recognizing that the reading (and later the writing of the response essay) begins with the reader, not the text or the author. In addition, by having students explore these questions, we are providing an entry point into their reading. Instead of contacting the book "cold," or with no warm-up activities, the students have been given a valuable opportunity to work their way gradually into the reading, a point Spack (1985, 1993) has made in discussing the link among literature, reading, and writing. This reader-based emphasis empowers students as L2 readers before what could be a complicated and at times frustrating reading experience. This approach places the *student as reader* on center stage and privileges her or his reading over any other aspects of the author/text/reader triangle.

As we accumulate more information and understanding through this process, we are better equipped to help our future students as well. The reader-based approach, then, also empowers us as L2 teachers. For instance, student responses may frequently show that their emphasis on locating the author's intended meaning is so strong that they can't feel empowered to respond with their own sense of authority. Knowing this can help teachers address this situation and create warm-up tasks that require students to focus on *their* views, not the intended meaning of the author.

Meanwhile, there is also much for students to gain if we read classroom discussions about the pre-reading questions. Sharing their pre-reading thoughts and questions may provide students with valuable reinforcement and encouragement, and encountering differences in ideas about reading among classmates from various linguistic and cultural backgrounds (assuming we have a heterogeneous classroom) will help students see how much reading originates within themselves, not with the assigned text.

Our post-reading questions stress the students' reading experience, not the text or authorial intention in it. We can ask a series of comprehension-type questions to explore students' understanding, of course, but we gain much more if we explore this vital realm of reading *experience,* not just reading comprehension. A focus on reading comprehension alone doesn't come close to telling the whole story about the students as readers, nor does it help us much in preparing the students to become better writers. An emphasis on reading comprehension tells us what students did and did not understand, but not *why* or *how* they performed as readers. For instance, reading comprehension tests won't necessarily tell us whether students relied on the bottom-up approach (in which readers pay particularly close attention to a text at the word and sentence level and probably consult dictionaries excessively, rather than focusing on creating a general or global understanding of what is taking place in the story). Reading specialists usually regard a heavy or exclusive emphasis on bottom-up reading as unhealthy for readers because the ability to read for larger meaning is lost. Hence, we need to know whether our students are depending on this or other reading strategies that may not be particularly effective. If we emphasize comprehension-based questions, we cannot delve into the level of understanding that a reader-response approach can provide.

Here are some of the reader-based questions that we can ask (and discuss) after the students have read the novel and that they can write about in, say, a journal:

1. Can you describe how you read the novel? What strategies or approaches did you use? Were they the same approaches you planned to use? If not, what changes did you make, and why? Did you try any strategies you use when reading novels in your native language?

2. What words or phrases would you use to describe your experience of reading *The Catcher in the Rye?* For example, was it a frustrating experience? A meaningful one?

3. What specific problems, if any, did you encounter while reading the story?

4. What were your opinions of Holden Caulfield as you read the novel and then when you finished it? Did

   your opinions/responses change while you read the
   story? If so, in what ways? Why? What specific
   words or phrases would you use to describe your
   responses to him?

5. What were your opinions of the novel itself as you
   were reading it and then when you finished it? Did
   your opinions/responses/emotions change? If so, in
   what ways? Why? What specific words or phrases
   would you use to describe your responses to the
   novel?

6. What kinds of writing, if any, did you do while
   reading the novel? For example, did you write any
   notes? Did you write in the margins of the book's
   pages? Do you think that this writing while reading
   helped prepare you to write your response essay?

7. Now that you have read the story and have to write
   your essay, what do you think the phrase *response
   essay* means? Have you formed any new ideas about
   this phrase since you began reading the novel?

8. Choose the section of the novel that you reacted to
   most strongly and describe how you read and
   responded to that section. Why did that section
   affect you more than others? Did you read it more
   than once? Did you write notes or in some other way
   use writing while you read it?

9. What were your reactions to the end of the novel?
   Were you disappointed? Happy? Would you change
   it in any way if you could?

The answers to these questions, like those to the pre-reading questions, should be of considerable help to us as teachers, especially as we prepare students for the writing phase of
the assignment. By looking so deeply into how the students
have read the story and how they attempted to construct responses to the novel and to Holden Caulfield, we gain a better understanding of their preparations for and potential prob-

lems with the writing of the essay and can of course gear our teaching to addressing any concerns that arise.

At the same time, by directing attention to the students' reading strategies and other aspects of their reading experience, we have reinforced, for students, the crucial idea that their participation in the novel as readers is of central importance. We will be telling them that reading in the L2 is not simply a matter of mechanically decoding the meaning of words and sentences or trying to locate meaning the author has intended to convey. Instead, we will tell them that *they* bring something vital to the reading experience and that what they contribute as readers matters greatly. In this way we can hopefully begin to communicate to them the all-important idea that reading is a productive, meaning-making activity in the same way that writing about their reading is. Then, too, by focusing on their performance as readers, we help draw attention to the composing processes that constitute both reading and writing, and in the process, we contribute to students' development as readers and writers. Our reader-response emphasis is what makes this possible.

A College Scenario

At the comminity college or college level, whether in an ESL writing course or a course such as mandatory first-year composition, there will likely be focus on academic writing of the kind required in other college courses. One task commonly assigned is summary writing. In ESL courses this is an especially valuable assignment because "summarizing tasks are junctions where reading and writing encounters take place and it is here that a complex composing process begins" (Sarig, 1993, p. 161). Assigning this kind of task allows us to both explore and develop our students' knowledge and skills as readers and writers. However, summaries tend to pose certain difficulties for NNS writers. For one thing, what exactly does it mean to summarize a text? Notions of summarization may vary from culture to culture, and our students of course bring with them knowledge of writing in their native language as well as in English, as discussed earlier. This knowledge can affect not only how they write their summary in English but how they read the assigned source text(s). Our students' knowledge of text structures in their L1 may influence how they read in the L2 in the sense of shaping what they look for and where in the text they look for it. An example might be the thesis statement, that is, the statement of the text's main idea. In some languages the thesis may more frequently be found early in the text; in others it may occur more often at or near the end. Its degree of directness in stating the purpose of the text may also vary. These differences might cause confusion for our students, in that they might miss the thesis because of where they expect to find it and how they expect it to look. If they miss the thesis, the writing of the summary will be extremely difficult, and the summary produced may then be ineffective or inappropriate. Here, once again, we see how a writing problem can be traced back to a reading problem, or, rather, to a reading practice that doesn't match the writing purpose at hand.

Let's suppose the students have been asked to write a one-paragraph objective summary for each of three newspaper and magazine articles on the subject of cloning. It is very possible that these texts will not be read in a neutral or objective fashion by the students. For one thing, the students may have their own cultural/religious views on this controversial subject and may then read the texts through the filter of those views. Then there is the potential problem discussed earlier: students may have notions of summary writing and of reading and text organization at variance with expectations and rhetorical practices in an Anglophone university setting. The net result could be a significant mismatch between, on the one hand, how the students approach both the reading and writing involved in the assignment and, on the other, what the teacher expects of them. How can a reader-response approach help in these circumstances? The main task here will be to focus on the students as readers *before* they begin the reading/writing process. Here are some of the questions they could be asked to write about or discuss in a pre-reading exercise:

1. What do you think is required in an English summary of a text? What does the word *summary* mean to you? What does it mean to write an "objective" summary? What makes it objective? What, in your view, must be included in a good objective summary of a text?
2. Have you written summaries in your native language? What are the main features of a summary written in your language? As far as you can tell, are there differences between summaries in your native language and in English?
3. How do you plan to read these three articles on cloning? What reading strategies will you use? What will you look for when you read the articles? Will the fact that you will be writing an objective summary of the articles have any effect on how you read the articles?
4. What does the key term *cloning* mean? Do you feel comfortable with a term like *human genetic engineering?* If one term sounds better to you, why? And what are some of your thoughts about cloning? Do you think your views on cloning will have any effect on how you read the assigned articles?
5. What writing, if any, will you do while you read the assigned articles? And what will you do with this writing after you finish reading the articles? Do you think writing while reading is helpful?

These questions, like those in the high school scenario, are intended partly to maneuver the students into seeing themselves, not the texts or the authors of the texts, as the starting point in the reading process. This approach will hopefully suggest to them that *they*, not the texts, control the reading process, especially if there are opportunities for students to share their answers with each other. Comparing their answers with each other will highlight their own role as the starting point in reading. Their answers will also provide valuable feedback for the teacher in terms of understanding how the students will approach the assignment. Such knowledge will (a) make it easier for teachers to address potential reading and writing problems or mistakes before they occur and (b) help teachers understand, while they read students' summaries, the possible origin of writing problems the students may have experienced. For example, a teacher might learn that her students see little or no value in writing while they read. Awareness of this tendency will make it easier for the teacher to prepare students to write while they read, for example, by demonstrating her own writing while reading.

The reader-based approach better prepares students to face the reading-writing task at hand by creating meaningful ground on which students can discuss or explore what they are going to do. Rather than throwing them into a complex task they may be unprepared to face, we pave the way for them to perform their reading and writing in informed ways. As in the scenario involving *The Catcher in the Rye,* they enter the reading experience with some preparation for it and so are better positioned to engage the source texts meaningfully.

Students can also be asked a series of reader-based or reading-based post-reading questions aimed at exploring the students' experiences while reading. Here, again, the emphasis would be not on comprehension of the source texts (though there is room in modified reader-response approaches for some examination of comprehension) but, rather, on student experiences of the texts. Questions that could be asked follow:

1. Did you read each of the three articles the same way? If not, why were there any differences in your readings? What were the differences?
2. As you read the articles, did you find that your own

thoughts on cloning affected your reading in any way? If so, how?

3. To what extent did you think about your summary writing exercise as you read the articles? Did you look for what you felt were important sentences or ideas that you could use in your summary?

4. Did you find any influence of your native language reading strategies while you read the articles? If so, which one(s)?

Class discussion of the answers to these questions, as with discussion of the questions we saw earlier, would likely reveal differences in students' reading experiences. Awareness of these differences would help draw students' attention to the individual meaning-making activities they engaged in as readers. This, in turn, would help students understand the role *they* play in reading, as opposed to focusing only on the role the texts play. Without this reading-based focus generated by a reader-response orientation, such understanding would be much more difficult to obtain, and the reading side of the summary writing exercise would likely end up undervalued and misunderstood.

Conclusion

Grabe and Kaplan (1996) remind us that "reading and writing are reciprocal activities; the outcome of a reading activity can serve as the input for writing, and writing can lead a student to further reading resources" (p. 297). As teachers of writing, we need to help our students understand this notion of the reciprocity between reading and writing in order to enhance both their reading and writing skills. Brozo (1988) notes that "proponents of reader-response and writing . . . contend that students become more actively involved in reading when they are led to see that they have a role in determining meaning. They become more conscious of alternative perspectives, and they improve their ability to learn from text" (p. 141). And as they learn from text—for example, becoming more familiar with commonly used rhetorical strategies in the target language writing—they extend their composing processes as writers.

Assuming that teachers do decide to work at least in part from a reader-oriented perspective, in what ways would a reader-response approach influence L2 writing instruction? To better understand the pedagogical implications and benefits of a reader-response approach, we can briefly picture a writing classroom that does not account appropriately for reading and readers. Here we can look again at the classroom scenarios cited earlier. Many teachers may conceptualize the assignments only or principally as writing tasks (even though there must be reading of the assigned texts) and thus focus only on teaching students techniques for organizing the kinds of texts they are writing. The writing submitted by students is then assessed according to how well the guidelines for the assignments have been followed. In these circumstances, there has been no accounting for the complex act or set of acts involved in reading the source texts and moving information acquired through reading them into writing, even though it was reading that initiated and helped guide the assignment sequences. Composing is assumed to have begun with writing, and problems in writing the response essay or summary paragraphs are then conceived of as writing problems. In truth, and as has already been explained, those writing problems *may* originate in reading problems or complexities arising from L1-based reading practices or other causes, and these may be rooted in the composing processes employed (or not employed) by students during the reading of the source text(s). Without some degree of focus on reading and students' reading experiences, then, teachers might unfairly assess the writing received and do both themselves and their students a disservice.

As we saw in the instructional scenarios described earlier in this chapter, a teacher following a reader-response approach would begin the assignments with an interest in the students as *readers* and a recognition that the students will bring their own composing resources into their reading of the source texts. There would be an understanding that not all the students would read the texts in the same way or even define the terms *response* or *summary* in the same way. Efforts would then be made to explore student intentions, assumptions, beliefs, and so forth, regarding the reading and writing to follow and perhaps after the students have completed their reading and writing.

The response and summary writing scenarios just described can be extended to any of the tasks that writing instructors assign and teach and that involve reading of source texts. The thesis of this chapter and this book is that such tasks should be treated as assignments in which reading and writing are connected to, not separated from, each other. Because it is perhaps natural for writing teachers to emphasize the writing-based dimensions of the assignment, the reading experience that serves as the starting point for the task and helps compose the writing that follows may be ignored completely or dealt with insufficiently by the instructor. We've demonstrated that by working from a reader-response perspective, an instructor would assume that a writing task *is* a reading task and that the student is not a neutral reader when engaging the assigned text(s). Both students and teachers benefit when we place at least some emphasis on students' meaning-making experiences as readers. The reader-response approach moves reading and the student as reader to a place in classroom practice where space is shared equally with writing. Inspired and guided by a reader-response orientation, readers and reading would emerge from the shadows of the writing classroom and be privileged as vital components in the teaching of writing and in students' activity as writers.

Questions for Reflection and Discussion

1. To what extent do you agree with the statements early in this chapter that "good writers are good readers" and "good readers are good writers"; that is,

do you agree with either or both of those statements? Why?

2. Adopting a reader-response pedagogy means that a teacher relinquishes at least some control over interpretations made of assigned texts and accepts students as partners in that process of interpretation. How comfortable will you be, as a teacher, with this idea?

3. How do you think your students would react to Leki's statement (quoted on p. 48) that "a text is not a puzzle or a dictator; it is a partner in a dialogue, in a negotiation"? What's your own reaction to this statement?

4. Reader-response theory has generally been applied to the reading of literary texts. To what extent can it be a useful tool when dealing with nonliterary texts? What circumstances would govern its effective use with nonliterary texts?

5. Because reader-response theory may be a challenging or difficult concept for some students to fully understand or accept, what would be some good activities to prepare them for exposure to it?

6. Is reader-response theory equally effective with respect to working with texts in the L1 and the L2? Or does it have more use or appeal in just one language context (L1 or L2)? Why?

7. What are the implications of a reader-response pedagogy with respect to assessment of student writing? Will it create assessment problems or assessment opportunities?

8. This chapter has asserted that reader-response theory will enhance the development of L2 reading-writing connections. What arguments can be made against that belief?

Chapter 3

Writing to Read

Chapter 1 discussed the research and perspectives that form the foundation for portraying reading and writing as closely related acts drawing on many of the same composing skills. Chapter 2 showed how reader-response theory can serve as a valuable bridge between reading and writing and open important doors for investigating and teaching reading-writing relationships. However, our focus in Chapter 2 was primarily on how, through reader-response theory, **teachers** can benefit from investigations of reading-writing relations in the sense of using reader-response theory to acquire important information about their students as readers and writers (in L1 and L2 contexts). In chapter 3 we shift our focus to some extent toward the ways in which **students** can experience and benefit from classroom work that links reading and writing, as well as how teachers can approach the process of building relationships between writing and reading.

In this chapter it will be important to understand that characterizing reading and writing as similar meaning-making processes, as was the case in the first two chapters, can in some regards be misleading at the same time that it is a fundamental way in which to view the interaction between reading and writing; that is, it may imply that they always act *equally* on each other. In fact, from an instructional point of view, we may gain more by drawing certain distinctions between them while at the same time bearing in mind their core similarities. In particular, we can look at how writing *supports* reading (the focus of this chapter) and how reading *supports* writing (the focus of Chap. 4).

Eisterhold (1990), in a synthesis of research on L1 reading-writing relationships, sees three interrelated models for such relationships and offers ideas on how they can be applied to investigations and teaching of L2 reading-writing connections.

- According to the *directional model,* knowledge from one of these skills can be transferred to and thus inform the other. The example given is of a student reading a comparison-contrast essay and using the knowledge gained from that exposure through reading to shape the writing of the same kind of essay. The key feature of this model, she says, is that "this transfer of structural information can proceed only in one direction" (p. 89), that is, from reading to writing (as in the comparison-comparison example just cited) or from writing to reading (in other situations). In these circumstances, she says, reading provides input for writing *or* writing provides input for reading.
- The *nondirectional model,* which works from the same assumption as the directional model—that reading and writing share common features—says that transfer between the skills can move in both directions, rather than just one, as in the directional model. Given the underlying belief that "reading and writing are said to derive from a single underlying proficiency, the common link being that of the cognitive process of constructing meaning," she adds that "since there is a single cognitive proficiency underlying both reading and writing, improvement in one domain will result in improvement in the other" (p. 90). (By contrast, improvement occurs in just one direction in the directional model).
- The third model, the *bidirectional model,* does not look at reading and writing as just interactive in nature but posits that they "are interdependent as well" (p. 92). In other words, reading *is* writing, and writing *is* reading, in which case the development of each skill must affect the other as well. However, the improvement may be

more complicated than in the nondirectional hypothesis, in that it may be experienced to different degrees and in different ways during the various stages of development.

While these models arise from L1 reading-writing research, Eisterhold asserts that they offer "the second language writing teacher a valuable perspective on reading-writing interactions in the writing classroom" (p. 93).

Chapters 3 and 4 focus on the directional model, one in which students are encouraged to use reading to help writing and/or writing to help reading. This focus is not meant to minimize the value of the nondirectional and bidirectional models. Rather, such an emphasis is in line with Eisterhold's assertion (in the same 1990 essay) that "this directional perspective is the relevant one for pedagogical concerns, since it helps teachers decide whether reading should precede writing in the classroom or whether writing should precede reading" (p. 89). For writing teachers, this is an important decision in terms of its influence on assignment and course design and in its impact on students' learning. As writing teachers, we need to know in which direction we wish to enhance students' development of literacy skills: from reading to writing or writing to reading. In Chapter 4, we'll look at research and teaching possibilities in the *reading-for-writing* mode in which reading precedes (and in the process informs or influences) writing. In this chapter we'll examine *writing for reading,* where writing precedes (and thus shapes or directs) reading.

Defining Writing to Read

Writing to read. . . . .
Writing for reading. . . . .
Writing while reading. . . . .

These commonly used phrases all lead to the core principle at the heart of the notion of writing to read: that writing before, during, or after reading enables a reader to make sense of her or his reading, which in turn strengthens the quality of the reading and contributes to the development of L2 reading skills. We can return briefly to the teaching scenario used in Chapter 2 to illustrate this point and, in the process, define the phrase *writing to read.* Recall how students reading the popular novel *The Catcher in the Rye* by J. D. Salinger (1951) could employ a reader-response approach to enrich their reading of the story. Let's now imagine a more specific setting involving the novel.

Suppose an ESL student—in middle school, high school, or college—has just finished reading the second chapter of the novel. In that chapter, Holden Caulfield visits one of his teachers after learning that he (Holden) is being forced to leave the private school he's been attending. As Holden is walking away from his teacher, Mr. Spencer, he believes he hears Mr. Spencer shouting "Good luck!" to him. The chapter ends with Holden rather mysteriously telling his readers, "I'd never yell 'Good luck!' at anybody. It sounds terrible, when you think about it" (p. 16). However, he doesn't tell us why this is terrible (or why we should think about it). At this point in the story, we hardly know Holden, and these comments are not likely to help us understand him. If anything, they might make him more difficult to understand. Meanwhile, this is the conclusion to a chapter, and that positioning in a novel is often used to prepare or situate readers for an important event to come in the next or a later chapter or to place the just completed chapter in focus. In this case, though, we're left with a mystery, because the comment doesn't appear to shape anything that will be helpful to us as readers. Readers can ignore that mystery and ignore Holden's comment, or they can try to make some sense of it out of a belief that it might have some importance in the development of the story.

Without necessarily thinking their decision through consciously, many readers may turn to writing as a means of doing something with that strange ending. They may sense, instinctively, that writing something at that point, such as jotting notes in the margin, may help them in some way. These might be questions—for example, "What's going on?" "What does Holden mean here?" "What's wrong with wishing someone good luck?" "What does this tell us about Holden?" "Why does Holden want us to know this?" Or students may record, in a journal or some place in the book itself, some possible interpretations of those lines or comments about Holden himself. What's happening here is that they're using writing to probe what they have read so as to lend clearer shape to the reading. Something—prior writing experience or intuition—may lead almost naturally to the notion that writing, which is a concrete act, begins to make visible the invisible or semivisible. Of course, they could raise the preceding questions in their mind as well, but by recording them in writing (say, in the margins of the text), they engage the text more directly. The physical act of writing creates a kind of contact point with the text and brings perceptions and impressions half formed during reading out of the shadows and into the light of emerging understanding. Then, too, by being written down, these questions (and tentative answers also recorded in the margins or some other place) don't go away. They await readers every time they happen to revisit the end of Chapter 2, and they position readers' entrance into Chapter 3.

The act of writing down one's questions, ideas, and so forth, allows readers to pause and think about what they have read thus far rather than, in the case of this example, rushing into Chapter 3 of the novel without direction. Indeed, any answers readers generate may then shape their future reading of the story as they seek confirmation of their early hypotheses about the character of Holden Caulfield. Vivian Zamel, in her seminal reading-writing connections article "Writing One's Way into Reading" (1992), summarizes the effects of such writing when she explains that "the heuristic nature of writing allows one to discover and consider one's stance, one's interpretation, one's immediate reactions to a text. Moreover, it makes these responses to a text overt, concrete, and tangible" (p. 470). She goes on to point out that "though we may not always respond in writing to our texts, when we underline portions of texts, mark them up, stop and verbalize our reactions, or scribble marginal comments, we are using interpretive strategies that give us insight into our meaning making" (pp. 470–471).

Let's also consider what we and our students do when reading materials for academic purposes. Suppose our students are preparing for a history test. As they read their textbook or article, they might write short summaries or annotations in the text's margins or in some other place, pencil in translations in their first language, write about how a point just raised links to something else written in another part of the text, or use another act of writing common among students in relation to their reading. Without these acts, their reading may proceed in a haphazard manner, or they may find it difficult to remember what they have read. We follow the same principle when we annotate material we read for teaching or other purposes, especially in order to explore or probe what we have read. These annotations help guide our reading, as well as our rereading when we revisit that material in a subsequent reading. Without any conscious thought, we—and our students—intuitively understand that writing, even in such related acts as highlighting or underlining sentences, helps or supports our reading.

We can look at my preparations for writing this chapter of this book as one more example of writing to read. As with other chapters in the book, I read widely among the related professional literature. Had I simply focused on reading that material without the support of writing, my reading would have become unfocused, and in all likelihood important points would have been lost. Instead, I used writing regularly to monitor and organize my reading. For example, while reading or reviewing the literature, I copied onto 3 x 5" index cards what I saw as important quotes or points, wrote notes about potential ways of categorizing ideas concerning writing to read, wrote summaries of what seemed to be especially important works in this area, drafted and redrafted outlines of the chapter as my notions of it took on new directions, and so forth. As this writing took place, my reading (and rereading) became more focused, and as it became more focused, it became more effective as well. All along the way, I wasn't writing to write; I was writing to construct more sensible and useful *readings* of the material I had gathered. It's also important to note that I wrote *while* reading and *after* reading. In each case, writing served as a means of creating better reading—and better reading hopefully has led to better writing. Linda Blanton (1993) makes a similar point in describing how she began a paper she wrote about reading-writing connections, when she observes that "we don't know what we've read until we begin to work with it by talking and writing about it" (p. 241). Sorting out her reading through writing brought that reading into clearer focus and in turn empowered her writing.

Writing to read, then, can be defined as the use of writing at various stages of reading to ensure stronger reading, with writing serving as a *means,* a tool, not an end or final activity. As we will see later in this chapter, this writing can take numerous forms. One of our tasks as writing teachers can be to introduce these forms to our students.

Origins of Writing to Read

In this section we look briefly at where notions of writing to read have come from, as this kind of background will help us better understand the contributions a writing-to-read framework can make to our pedagogy and to our students' acquisition of academic literacy.

Common Sense

To a certain extent, the idea of writing to read probably comes from instinct or common sense, as suggested earlier. Intuitively, and then through experience, we understand that writing has a unique power to bring clarity to our thoughts, to soothe our nerves, to provide new ways of examining situations, to allow us to review alternative interpretations of events, and so forth. This idea is reflected in Burnham and French's (1999) observation that "oftentimes, we are able to make sense of our experience only insofar as we are able to represent it to ourselves" (p. 77). We do that principally (or at least frequently) through writing. That's partly why diary or journal writing is so popular. The writing of a diary provides comfort and insight that might otherwise be difficult to obtain, especially amid complicated or highly emotional experiences in our daily lives. The same is true for, say, constructing outlines before writing a paper. The act of writing enables us to better visualize how we want the paper to proceed. Relying strictly on thought, on thinking through the ways in which we might organize the paper, doesn't work well for many of us. It certainly wouldn't have worked for me in writing this chapter. Along these lines, John Gage (1986) draws the distinction between thought and writing in the following explanation:

> One difference, of course, between writing and thinking is that writing is tangible—it results in a finite product—while thinking is intangible, and just goes on and on (or, sometimes, around and around). . . . Writing is thinking-made-visible, thinking that can be examined because it is "on the page" and not all "in the head," invisibly floating around. Writing is thinking that can be stopped and tinkered with. It is a way of making thought hold still long enough to examine its structures, its possibilities, its flaws. The road to clearer understanding of one's own thoughts is traveled on paper. It is through the attempt to find words for ourselves, and to find patterns for ourselves in which to express related ideas, that we often come to discover exactly what we think. (p. 24)

Knowing that in many cases thinking about what we have read or experienced isn't enough to ensure full or satisfactory understanding, we intuitively look for a way to record (and perhaps analyze) in writing what we have encountered in life experiences and in reading that is important to us for one reason or another. With regard to education, Vacca, Vacca, and Gove (1991) emphasize the commonsense aspect of writing to read when they observe, in looking at teaching reading at the elementary school level, that "common sense tells us that writing is intended to be read. When children are writing, they can't help but be involved in reading" (p. 137). In this way, writing draws greater attention to reading, since it must be read during and probably after the writing takes place.

Critiques of Reading Instruction

Notions of writing to read and its use in classroom instruction also come from powerful critiques of the ways in which reading is often taught, at least in the United States. Perhaps the most famous and enduring critique of reading instruction at the earliest level of education is found in Rudolf Flesch's controversial and still frequently cited book from the mid-1950s, *Why Johnny Can't Read* (1955), and reiterated in his equally controversial follow-up, *Why Johnny* Still *Can't Read* (1981). Flesch observed that many American schoolchildren have been taught to read individual words without an understanding of the system by which words are constructed; that is, they are taught to read in a kind of vacuum. He cites, for example, the idea of teaching students set numbers of words at different levels of schooling, as if reading is simply a matter of acquiring individual words. In addition to advocating, as an alternative, an approach resembling the controversial phonics movement, he asserted that

> the best way to learn any system [of language] is to learn to write and to read it at the same time. And how do you do that? The obvious answer is, By taking up one symbol after another and learning how to write it and how to recognize it. Once you are through the whole list of symbols, you can read and write; the rest is simply practice—learning to do it more and more automatically. (1981, p. 3)

In short, writing is part of the foundation of reading and so should be used to teach reading. Flesch supports his argument by citing the learning of other language systems such as shorthand, Morse code, and Braille. In his words, "nobody learns how to *read* shorthand. People who want to know shorthand learn how to *write* it; the reading of it comes later" (1981, p. 3). His point is that we learn those systems of language first by writing them, so why not learn to read our everyday language in the same way? Perfetti & Zhang (1996) explain that "learning to read, whatever else it is, is a question of *learning*. And what is learned is the workings of a writing system and specific orthography" (p. 40). Hence, writing is a key entry point into reading and should be emphasized in the teaching of reading. Indeed, Vacca, Vacca, and Gove (1991) assert that "there is compelling evidence to suggest that writing and reading abilities develop concurrently and should be nurtured together" (p. 126).

Criticisms of reading instruction at later stages of education point out other problems. Leki (1993), for example, explains that through the common approach of teaching cognitive reading strategies, students "are still not learning reading; they are learning strategies for reading which can at best be only imitations of reading behavior, like children turning the pages of books they cannot yet read" (p. 15). Zamel (1992) identifies another problem: "The way reading gets taught (and evaluated) in schools tends to keep hidden from students the sense making and exploration that makes reading possible and that, in turn, reading makes possible. What is practiced in the guise of reading suggests to students that reading is a receptive and static process, rather than an active, participatory one involving the dynamic contributions of a reader" (pp. 463–464). Then there is the criticism offered by Donald Bartholomae and Anthony Petrosky in their book *Ways of Reading* (1987), the text for one of the most famous college-level integrated reading-writing courses in the United States. As they explain at the beginning of the book: "Our students . . . felt powerless in the face of serious writing, in the face of long and complicated texts—the kinds of texts we thought they should find interesting and challenging" (p. iii). They summarized their assessment of this situation in another book that has heavily influenced the joint teaching of reading and writing, *Facts, Artifacts, and Counterfacts* (1986): "Their [students'] problems, we concluded, were not intrinsically reading problems but problems of composing, the ability to 'compose' a reading" (p. 23). In these two books, they describe a number of writing-for-reading strategies designed to instantiate in students the composing ability essential in reading and learned through writing. At the heart of their pedagogy is the belief that it is writing which can remove, or reduce, that sense of powerlessness as readers some students experience.

Writing to Learn

A third major influence on the development of writing-to-read strategies—and a crucial link between reading and writing—is the writing-to-learn movement, the basis on which the writing-across-the-curriculum movement was developed. Writing to learn has it roots in various ways of looking at the processes of learning. For instance, as Kucan and Beck (1997) note in a review of "thinking aloud" literature, research has long shown that asking students to talk about what they have read impacts positively on their reading comprehension. Writing to learn is based on the notion that writing has similar, if not stronger, effects on learning, as Vacca and Linek (1992) point out when they observe that "to find meaning and purpose in learning, students must be encouraged to think about what they are learning—and therein lies the power of writing" (p. 145). This is in large part because, as Janet Emig asserted in her groundbreaking essay "Writing as a Mode of Learning" (1977), "Writing serves learning uniquely because writing as a process-and-product possesses a cluster of attributes that correspond uniquely to certain powerful learning strategies" (p. 122), a point echoed in another of the early and important papers on writing to learn, Lee Odell's "The Process of Writing and the Process of Learning" (1980). Schumacher and Gradwohl Nash (1991) provide an additional perspective underlying writing to learn, when they note that "it is widely believed that writing plays an important role in knowledge change" (p. 92); that is, through various writing activities, students can transform the knowledge they obtain (especially via reading) to serve other purposes requiring applications of that knowledge. Furthermore, as Soven explains in her popular writing-across-the curriculum textbook *Write to Learn* (1996), "The act of writing enhances knowing: retrieving information, organizing it, and expressing it in writing seems to improve understanding and retention" (p. 1). Thus, says Herrington (1981), "writing has an integral role to play in any course as a medium of learning and for teaching how to learn" (p. 387), especially in the context of writing-across-the-curriculum activities.

The ideas just expressed helped lead to the use of writing in courses besides English courses as a means of allowing students to process their learning in other subjects, such as biology and history. And because reading is so often a central activity in these content courses, writing came to be seen as a means of enabling students to unravel or make sense of that reading. Later in this chapter we'll look at specific applications of the core notion of writing to learn in linking reading and writing. For now we simply need to understand that writing has come to be seen as a tool of learning, not as an end in itself. As Zamel (1992) explains in summarizing the idea of writing to read and to learn, "Writing, because it gives students opportunities to discover that reading is an active and generative process, teaches students a critical lesson about reading. It allows students not just to learn about something in a particular text, but to learn about how one learns" (p. 481). This includes how one reads. Jane Hansen captures the essence of this point when she observes, in her popular book on teaching reading to children, *When Writers Read* (1987), that "writing is the foundation of reading; it may be the most basic way to learn about reading" (p. 178).

While, as noted earlier, the writing-to-learn theory and research has heavily influenced the development of the writing-across-the-curriculum movement, it has also played a role in the formation of the currently popular (and controversial) whole language movement. Sarah Hudelson, in her book

Write On: Children Writing in ESL (1989), illustrates this point in the following observation:

> Whole language educators maintain that learners do not first learn to read and write and then learn school content. Rather, as learners explore topics of interest to them, they naturally engage in reading and writing about these topics. It is through such engagement that literacy develops. Students become readers and writers and learn more about written language and about the power of literacy by carrying out meaningful reading and writing activities. (p. 47)

While these comments also point to the value of using reading to support or improve writing, we can view them here as a further pretext for employing writing as a tool for reading, both in teaching reading itself and in using writing and reading in helping L2 students acquire academic literacy skills necessary in their content courses. In the rest of this chapter we'll see applications of the ideas discussed thus far in accounts of both L1 and L2 writing instruction, after first reviewing major research focused on writing in relation to reading and learning.

Writing to Read/Learn Research

Most of the research examining the effects of writing on learning and reading has been in the L1 domain. (Noteworthy reviews of this research are found in Ackerman, 1993; Geisler, 1995; Many, Lewis, & Mitchell, 1996; McGinley & Tierney, 1989; Newell, 1998; Schumacher & Gradwohl Nash, 1991; and Sternglass, 1993). Reviewers point out that research in this this area has identified positive effects in the use of writing to enhance learning and reading, especially when the writing takes the form of longer and more analytic texts (as opposed to short exercises). However, a reservation that appears across reviews is that the writing-to-learn situation is a far more complex one than was originally believed, leading to shortcomings in much of the research. According to Newell (1998), "The problem is that we have focused on an ap proach to teaching and learning without asking the more difficult question of what is worth knowing and why" (p. 199). Furthermore, as McGinley and Tierney (1989) point out, such research has been narrowly focused, so that "these studies provide a somewhat limited picture of how students might use more complex combinations of reading and writing en route to thinking and learning" (p. 245), especially with regard to the development of critical-thinking skills. Still, valuable insights have been gained into those activities that help and/or hinder the use of writing to enhance learning and reading.

To a lesser extent, these studies have focused on writing to read and learn in literature courses (e.g., Marshall, 1987; Newell, Suszynski, & Weingart, 1989). For the most part, though, the emphasis has been on writing used for learning (and thus for reading) in the sciences, social sciences, and history (e.g., Greene, 1993; Langer, 1986; Newell, 1984; Newell & Winograd, 1989, 1995; Smagorinsky, 1997; Sternglass, 1993; Tierney, Soter, O'Flahavan, & McGinley, 1989). One of the major findings of relevance to this chapter is that more complex writing tasks involving some degree of composing (e.g., analytic and response-based essays) have a greater impact on students' learning than do less demanding activities such as note taking and answering study questions (Newell, 1984). Another finding of interest for this chapter is that what Greene (1993) calls "extended writing" (e.g., long reports and problem-solving essays) helps learning more than shorter, less challenging writing tasks. In general terms, says Marshall (1987), "If both writing and reading are viewed as constructive processes, then writing about reading should provide students with an opportunity to 'enrich and embellish' the meanings they have tentatively constructed, coming to a fuller possession of whatever the text may hold" (p. 31).

Thus far there has been less emphasis on research into uses of writing for reading in L2 teaching and learning situations.

As we'll see shortly, there is increasing interest in pedagogical applications of writing to read and learn strategies in L2 writing instruction, but few studies have examined writing-to-read and writing-to-learn. One of these, by Cumming (1990), looked at the effect of composing in a second language on second language acquisition and identified positive effects arising from such composing. A study by Connor and Mayberry (1996), while not aimed at investigating writing-learning connections, nevertheless concluded that a combination of reading, writing, and speaking (all acts of composing) is more likely to help L2 writers successfully negotiate a topic to be written about. Boughey (1997) examined 30 occupational therapy students using writing-to-learn strategies in group settings in a content course. She found that this application of the notion of writing to learn helped the participants in their language acquisition and in their understanding of the subject being studied. Writing in groups created valuable opportunities for the students to discuss, as they composed or prepared to compose papers, what they were reading as well as the language necessary for the reading and writing. Trudy Smoke's article "Writing as a Means of Learning" (1994) is another of the handful of L2 studies aimed directly at investigating the effects of writing on learning. Smoke conducted a longitudinal study of a college student named Ming to see how writing assisted her learning in courses other than writing classes. Smoke's case study confirmed what the Cumming study cited earlier did: as Ming's ability to write and her comfort level with writing in English improved, so did her general acquisition of English. Furthermore, as Smoke observes, "Ming's college writing experience was transformed by her discovery that she could use writing as a tool for learning" (p. 9). Ming was taking an ESL writing course for the sixth time when the study began, and it was when she began applying what she was learning there to a social science course she was taking (a course linked to the ESL course) that she began to understand the impact of writing on learning.

One other study worth noting, perhaps the most extensive to date on the writing-learning connection in an L2 context,

is Ruth Spack's article "The Acquisition of Academic Literacy in a Second Language" (1997). Spack tracked a student
named Yuko through three years of college-level study. Like
Ming in Smoke's study, Yuko struggled initially with her written English on entering college in the United States. She also
struggled in other courses. As the study progressed, however, Yuko gradually began to learn to use writing about her
course-related reading, particularly journal entries, to make
sense of the reading. This is reflected in Spack's summation
of Yuko's experiences in a particularly challenging sociology
class: "The experience of writing and revising journal entries
in her sociology class showed her a way to use writing to clarify reading and to put social scientists' ideas into her own
words" (p. 46).

Writing to Read in Classroom Contexts

This section examines the use of writing to support reading at
both a micro and macro level. From the micro perspective
we'll look at the principal writing modes and writing tasks in
which writing-to-read activities occur. We'll then enlarge the
focus to explore the writing-reading contexts in which these
activities most commonly take place.

Before we discuss these activities and contexts, we need to
briefly consider how students most frequently encounter
reading and writing—and the connections between them—in
school settings. Perhaps the common denominator here is
what we normally refer to as "sources" or "source texts," that
is, the materials students are assigned to read in search of important information about the subjects they are studying.
From the later years of elementary school through college and
in a variety of subjects, students are asked to read materials
that provide them with valuable information and ideas about
the subjects at hand. The professional literature uses such
terms as *composing from sources* and *writing from sources* to
frame the writing tasks students sometimes perform while using these materials, and Spack (1988) observes that "perhaps

the most important skill English teachers can engage students in is the complex ability to write from other texts, a major part of their academic writing experience" (pp. 41–42).

Because work with source texts begins with students' reading of them, the focus in textbooks and research is often on reading-for-writing strategies, since it is writing that serves as the end point or purpose of the reading, such as writing a term or research paper or a book report. However, as will become clear, composing from sources can also be approached from a writing-to-read perspective. For instance, as Gradwohl Nash, Schumacher, and Carlson (1993) point out, "Writing-from-sources tasks require several activities of the writer. These activities include choosing a topic, locating and evaluating sources, selecting information from the sources, and organizing and composing the essay" (p. 159). In this portrait of writing from sources, we see how writing can support and enhance reading, for example, in the evaluating, selecting, and organizing activities just mentioned, prior to the more involved act of writing a longer text based on the reading already performed. Thus, the main theme of this chapter is that conceptualizing composing from sources in this way can provide students with an invaluable entry point into the acquisition of L2 academic literacy skills and the combined use of reading and writing in developing and exercising such skills. We can see this more clearly by briefly examining a situation described in a case study by Schneider and Fujishima (1995). They investigated the academic literacy experiences of a graduate student named Zhang, who recorded the following thoughts in a journal he kept as part of their study:

> I discovered I had done wrong way for my researches because I was used to read a lot of articles and input my ideas, but I caught [?] a so widely that I could not focus on a field to research deeply. I think it is not only to narrow my researches, but also to narrow my ideas and my writing content. And depending on my information, I should have an outline and method to organize my idea and writing content. (p. 18).

Zhang is faced with what may be a standard reading-writing, or composing-from-sources, situation: he has to read several texts and then write in meaningful ways about them or use them to develop his ideas. We can see from his comments that Zhang recognized a weakness in his reading of the source texts. His problem was not necessarily overall comprehension but an inability to *do something* with the source texts. What's most interesting in his commentary is his understanding of the value of an outline or some kind of writing that would allow him to fit the pieces of his reading together before going on to the larger writing context in which he would use the texts as sources of data, quotations, theories, or whatever he would need from them. In short, Zhang implicitly recognized that he needed a way of writing about his reading while reading or just after reading, as an interim step between his reading of the source texts and whatever final form of writing he would perform with them. It is this kind of integrated reading-writing context that informs a point made by Carson and Leki (1993a): "Writing provides a way into reading, extends reading, and consolidates understanding of a text just as reading sustains writing and furnishes, for the writer, the counterpart of another voice" (p. 2). This is what Zhang needed and what many of our students need when asked to read and write about assigned source texts, at whatever level of education they find themselves: a means of reading not just for baseline comprehension of the texts but for establishing connections between texts, connections that, like the pieces of a jigsaw puzzle, make possible the assembly of the texts into something larger and more meaningful; that is, they need approaches to reading in which writing helps them make sense of the assigned source texts. These approaches will be discussed in the next section of this chapter.

Writing-for-Reading Activities

The activities we'll look at in this section are actually common to both the writing-for-reading and reading-for-writing instructional scenarios. However, how they are employed will differ depending on the mode—writing for reading or reading for writing—we need to emphasize in our instruction. Hence, while each activity will be discussed in both this chapter and Chapter 4, there will be significant differences in the nature of the discussions.

Summarizing

The writing of summaries, especially as a means to some larger writing end (e.g., summarizing several articles read for the eventual writing of a research paper), provides rich opportunities for writing to enhance reading and illustrates why it's so important to link reading and writing in L2 writing instruction. Indeed, summarizing is one of the primary contact points between reading and writing in academic settings, as students are either asked or on their own volition choose to write summaries for a wide variety of purposes across school subjects (e.g., history, biology, sociology) to demonstrate how well they understood what they were asked to read, to prepare for an examination, to help them acquire the most important knowledge or information in an assigned text, to keep track of a series of texts, and, as noted earlier, to prepare for a larger writing assignment. From elementary school through the highest levels of graduate school, students are likely to engage in summarizing at least from time to time.

Before looking at the role of reading and writing in summarizing and at the contribution writing makes to reading in this common learning context, let's get a clearer sense of what summarizing entails. Geisler (1995) says that "a summary is the simplest text that attempts to represent in some form what another text says" (p. 105). In his influential composition textbook *The Informed Writer* (1985), Bazerman explains that "summary, like paraphrase, allows you to reproduce another writer's thoughts—but in shortened form" (p. 67). During this process of reproduction, a student is called on to perform a variety of reading-writing tasks. For example, as Bazerman goes on to point out in his textbook, "In writing a summary, you focus on the most important statements of the original passage and eliminate the less important material. Four techniques—deleting, selecting, note taking, and miniaturizing—can help you shorten the material" (p. 67). At a more general level, Newell (1998) observes that "two types of plans are necessary for summarizing: plans for compressing and integrating information from the text and plans for representing the organization of the text in a succinct way" (p. 195).

If a student is attempting to summarize a relatively short and/or simple text, the activities just described can likely occur simply through careful reading of the source text. However, as the source texts involved become longer and more complex and as the purposes for which they are being read become more challenging (e.g., in the research paper example mentioned a moment ago), the act of reading effectively will probably become far more difficult for many L2 students. This is where writing can serve reading. If, for example, a student is reading a text several thousand words long and is struggling to make sense of the text, composing a summary and performing the kinds of activities previously described can add much-needed direction to the reading process. The reader's best chance to achieve meaningful comprehension (and later use) of the texts may rest in her or his ability to reduce the text to its main features and primary information in, for example, a 300-word summary of the original article. In part, this involves recognizing and eliminating what is not essential. This is, in effect, an act of composing, since the reader is basically creating a new and more manageable version of the original text, one reflecting her or his interpretation of what is and isn't important. However, composing that new text mentally, when there is so much source text content to process, is likely to be difficult for many L2 readers. There are probably going to be confusing or difficult moments in the text, causing the reader to generate questions as she or he proceeds through the text. In that case, the better option may be to turn to writing as a way of both recording and guiding the reconstruction of the text into a new and leaner text. As Zamel (1992) explains, linking writing to reading in such a case makes it possible for a reader to "resee texts and so lets us grapple with uncertainties, reflect on the complexities, deal with the puzzlements, and offer approximative readings. By providing us a means for working out a reading, writing allows insights that may have been inaccessible or inchoate at the time the text was read" (p. 472). It is in this vein that Zamel speaks of "writing one's way into reading."

In the case of summarizing, the writing-based subtasks that constitute summary writing—the deletion and selection and so forth already described—can allow the reader to see the source text(s) in more focused ways and minimize the frustration caused by trying to grasp a long and complicated text as a whole. In the act of summarizing, writing becomes an analytical tool serving the purposes of reading (which might, in turn, serve writing purposes later). In situations where we have reasons to expect our students to encounter difficulties while reading, adding a writing component such as summarizing might be the best reading gift we can give them.

Another benefit of using summary writing for reading-related purposes is that such writing provides teachers (and students) with a better understanding of students' reading processes and successes or difficulties. This is a message that emerges from the L2 summary writing research (e.g., Johns, 1985; Johns & Mayes, 1990; Kirkland & Saunders, 1991; Sarig, 1993), which has generally found that, regardless of students' L2 proficiency level, good summaries are difficult to produce, and to some extent such difficulty is linked to reading-related problems. By examining, in the written summaries, the students' choices in terms of what information has or has not been transferred from the source text to the summary and what passages from the original text students have chosen for paraphrasing, reading and writing researchers and teachers have gained deeper insight into students' L2 literacy skills and practices. "The summary," says Lent (1993), "becomes a revelation of whatever it is that connected for the reader" (p. 235). It also reveals what did not connect for the reader, and analysis of a student's summary may shed light on the problems that occurred during reading. Hence, summary writing can perform a diagnostic function for teachers and students, just as it can enrich students' reading.

To put summary writing as a writing-for-reading activity into greater perspective, let's turn to Sarig's (1993) observation that "summarizing tasks are junctions where reading and writing encounters take place" (p. 161), with reading being the first stage in those encounters. Whether that reading is intended to lead to writing of some kind, as is often the case in school settings, or whether the reading is intended for other purposes (e.g., taking a multiple-choice exam), we can make the reading experience more meaningful and productive for our students through summarizing tasks involving writing. Just as we can use writing to make sense of our experiences and conflicts in daily life through such activities as diary or journal writing, the composing processes involved in summary writing will enable students to encounter the texts they are reading in new ways—ways that will hopefully enable them to isolate the text's most important and valuable features and that will perhaps teach them lessons about L2 reading. Without this kind of support provided by writing, our students, as readers, may engage the act of L2 reading un- or underequipped to perform the act successfully. To paraphrase Zamel (1992), writing may be their best way into such reading. As we will see in the next subsection, that may be even truer in a higher order reading-writing task such as synthesizing, where students are required to work with more texts and create sophisticated connections between them.

Synthesizing

Like summarizing, synthesizing involves writing about source texts. It is also, like summarizing, a task students may well be expected to perform, particularly at the college level. However, where summaries are condensed reconstructions of individual texts, syntheses are discussions—especially through comparison and contrast—of two or more source texts at the same time. As Kennedy, Kennedy, and Smith (2000) explain in their popular composition textbook *Writing in the Disci-*

plines, "To synthesize is to select elements from two or more sources on a topic of interest that they share and then to organize them . . . under a controlling theme or idea. . . . you look for or create a controlling idea or thematic consistency" (pp. 93–94). In *The Informed Writer* (1985), Bazerman says that "the purpose of the essay of synthesis is to combine what a number of sources have to say into a coherent overview of the subject" (p. 261). Synthesizing, then, requires that readers/writers identify and explain issues, themes, relationships, and so forth, arising from more than one text. These are sophisticated acts of literacy in a native language and, as such, can pose particularly complex challenges for L2 readers and writers. At the same time, synthesizing, as a teaching and learning tool, provides rich opportunities for L2 students to develop their reading and writing abilities. By the same token, synthesizing is especially useful in drawing students' attention to connections between reading and writing (from both the writing-for-reading and reading-for-writing perspectives).

Synthesizing allows readers to use the same processes or activities of writing that we saw in the discussion of summarizing: extracting from the source texts important ideas or information, deleting unimportant material, and so forth. Where this kind of activity involves the reading-writing connection and allows writing to assist or support reading beyond summarizing is (a) in the increased options writers/readers have to appropriate material from the source texts and (b) in requiring even more focused use of writing to generate, while reading, the comparisons and contrasts and the relationships between texts central to synthesizing. Summaries of texts are meant to be short, condensed reconstructions of the original texts; syntheses, because they involve multiple texts, will be longer and more involved reconstructions. Writers thus have more room in which to draw material (especially in the form of paraphrases and quotations) from the original texts as they engage in the comparing, contrasting, and forging of relationships between the texts during and after reading.

Suppose, for example, that a high school or college student has been asked to write a report on AIDS research. This will usually necessitate reading at least a few articles and/or books on or visiting websites devoted to this topic. In order to compose a meaningful paper and to gain a deeper understanding of the topic, the student ultimately cannot (or should not) simply read each of these texts in isolation. That might be done initially, with the student perhaps then writing a short summary of each source text. At some point, though, the reader is going to have to assemble important and useful information from the texts into a meaningful whole. Creating this whole strictly through reading is probably a daunting task even for the best of readers. The more effective approach would be to try to synthesize these texts through some kind of analytic writing. The student can, for example, write notes about common themes or ideas she or he observes across the texts, either in the course of reading the texts or after reading them. The student could also use writing to build an outline that reconstructs the main points of the texts. Short summaries could also be written and then analyzed as a group of texts. In each of these cases, writing in some form of synthesizing plays a supporting role to reading. Writing paraphrases of key sentences and writing sentences that incorporate important quotations would also be helpful ways of using writing to strengthen reading, in that students would have to engage in especially close reading in order to paraphrase and quote successfully.

In fact, paraphrasing and quotation (both of which occur frequently in syntheses) are particularly interesting and meaningful activities in the context of reading-writing relations. In a study of 30 students' quotation practices, Campbell (1990) points out that paraphrasing and quoting from source texts are "processes that involve reading, understanding, learning, relating, planning, writing, revising, editing, and orchestrating" (p. 211)—processes in which reading and writing inevitably overlap and interact while the student locates and reconstructs or appropriates material from the source texts. This is why Murray, Parrish, and Salvatori (1998) assert that "quotations [and paraphrases] are at the threshold of reading and writing." Of course, not every sentence or longer passage in a text should be quoted or paraphrased. Selecting the most suitable material for quotation or paraphrasing requires careful reading of the source texts. Thus, by looking at what our students have and have not paraphrased and quoted, we learn more about the quality and nature of their reading. At the same time, analyzing the writing by which they have reframed the original source material in the form of a direct quotation or a paraphrase tells us more about their reading and writing abilities. From an instructional point of view, by assigning paraphrasing and quotation tasks, we can facilitate our students' reading of texts through the medium of writing, since it is through careful writing that the acts of paraphrasing and quotation occur. Here, too, then, we can reinforce the role that writing can play in the service of reading, that is, writing as a means, not an end. Meanwhile, the quoting and paraphrasing that take place in the course of synthesizing occur in a meaningful context, since they lead to the production of a paper on the topic assigned by the teacher. This is in contrast to the commonly assigned paraphrasing and direct quotation tasks in which writing teachers give students individual sentences and ask them to rewrite them as paraphrases or quotations, devoid of any larger contexts in which to situate the paraphrases and quotations. While there is value in such exercises, a meaningful understanding of reading connected to writing might not occur, since students have not had to select from a larger source text the sentences to be dealt with. Synthesizing tasks provide the context missing in such assignments, because students must quote and paraphrase according to some guiding principle or idea in deciding what to paraphrase or quote and how to do so in order to make the synthesis succeed.

Responding

Summarizing and synthesizing are generally seen as analytic or objective writing tasks in which the focus is on reconstructing the source texts without discussing one's own reactions to them. Their focus, as we have already seen, is on selecting, rejecting, extracting, and rearranging source text content. As beneficial as these activities are, they aren't the only ways for students to read through writing, or, rather, to use writing to read more effectively. Written responses to reading can also enhance reading, though from a different perspective than what we have seen thus far in this chapter. In responding to texts, where students focus on discussing their reactions to what they have read, the emphasis is on the *reading experience;* that is, through various kinds of response writing techniques, students essentially (and perhaps indirectly) tell a story of how they have read a text or texts. Blanton (1994) sees this as a process of students "talking to texts" (p. 10) rather than pulling information from them (as occurs in analytic writing). She also speaks of L2 students' "silence before a text" (1993, p. 236) and of the need to break that silence if reading is to proceed meaningfully. The more expressive writing that responding to texts entails puts the reader on center stage with the text(s), whereas the reader is on the sidelines to some extent while summarizing and synthesizing. Expressive writing, or responding, also creates opportunities for students to reflect on their learning or reading—what they have learned or read and/or how they have learned or read it—via writing (Vacca & Linek, 1992, p. 146). "Through writing," says Flynn (1982), "students gain a fuller understanding of their reading" (p. 149), because the act of responding to what they have read draws their attention to their performance as readers as they reengage the text(s) in search of ideas and material to respond to. In the next few pages, we'll look at some of the most commonly discussed forms of response in which there is a focus on using writing in support of reading.

Pre-Reading Writing

Some L2 writing specialists have emphasized the power and benefits of having students write before they read. Spack (1985, 1990, 1993), in particular, has examined the role of what she calls "write-before-you-read" activities in integrated reading-writing instruction, especially in the context of the reading of literary texts. Her approach features students writing freely (without concern for grammar or organization) for 10 to 15 minutes, with a focus on "their own experience about an idea or happening in the work they are about to read" (1985, p. 711). Leki (1993) describes the benefits of such an approach as follows: "Anticipating in writing the context of a text . . . primes schemata and thereby facilitates reading of a text" (p. 19). In other words, students avoid the common problem of approaching a text unprepared for it—and perhaps fearful of it—by having a personal frame of reference to work with as an entry point into the text, through having already situated themselves (tentatively, at least) relative to the text's major theme or framework. In this way, the text is less likely to be the intimidating stranger that texts in the target language often are to less proficient L2 readers. Ferris and Hedgcock (1998) discuss the use of such a writing-before-reading strategy when dealing with nonliterary texts. They ask students to explore, in advance of reading, the main issue or idea around which the text is developed. Here, too, writing allows the students to establish an entry point into or a connection with a text before they read it.

Response Statements

One of the key concepts fueling the reader-response pedagogy described briefly in Chapter 2 is David Bleich's notion of a "response heuristic," developed in his influential book *Subjective Criticism* (1978). This is a three-stage approach to teaching, in which students are asked to use writing to move from an initial description of what they saw as important in the text, to their responses, to what they observed, and then on to any associations they can make between events or information in the text and their own lives. The central component in this pedagogy is what he calls the *response statement.* He explains that "a response statement aims to record the perceptions of a reading experience and its natural, spontaneous consequences, among which are feelings, or affects, and peremptory memories or thoughts, or free associations" (p. 147). In this approach, then, students are asked to explore how they read the text rather than simply what they found in it. From the L2 perspective, and as we saw in Chapter 2, such experientially based accounts help teachers better understand their students as readers (and thus as writers). From the writing-for-reading perspective, response statements enable students to unravel, in their own terms, their stories of reading and thus to learn about themselves as readers as well as about the act of second language reading.

In analyzing one of his own response statements, for example, Bleich (1980) indicated that "I will understand this response statement as the representation of my reading" (p. 354), and it is this kind of written representation that can be useful in the L2 writing classroom as a means of improving reading. That's because the response statement, with its at least equal focus on the reader (rather than privileging the text), creates an opportunity for examining how the student read the text through the points made in the response statement. In order to enhance their value, Bleich asserts that such statements should not be graded and that students benefit from having teachers write and share them as well (p. 365). Leki (1993), too, has written of the value of writing teachers making "our own struggle with meaning visible by letting our students see our reading processes" (p. 24). This can be achieved by teachers composing and sharing with students their own response statements.

Each of these perspectives might be of particular value in L2 writing instruction, in that students may write more freely—and thus explore their reading more meaningfully—without the pressure of knowing their writing will be assessed, and they can derive both pleasure and meaning from learning about their teachers' stories of reading. Regardless of whether response statements are perceived in the classroom as pieces of writing standing on their own or as the initial stage of a larger writing experience, they provide teachers and students with invaluable insight into the ways in which students read (Petersen, 1982, p. 460). At the same time, writing is once again seen as a tool in the reading process, not as a skill existing separately from reading.

Response Essays

Like response statements, response essays concentrate on a student's reading experience. However, they can move beyond the primary emphasis on interpretation of a text or of a reading experience found in response statements. For instance, Salvatori (1996) asks her students to compose a "difficulty paper" in which, as the name suggests, they concentrate on describing where they encountered problems in their reading. This kind of essay then creates meaningful opportunities for classroom discussion of ways of removing or minimizing those difficulties. In addition, says Lent (1993):

> The response paper is a way of breaking the silence between the text and the student; it brings to words the solitary activity of student-with-reading, and, at the same time, becomes a means of empowerment. Having written something down about the text gives a student "authority" over it, and this in turn seems to provide the confidence to speak out in class. (p. 233)

Another significant aspect of response essays is that, while they need not be formal or graded papers, they often require that students cite passages from the assigned text to support or illustrate points made in their writing. Lent adds: "A student can express anything in it so long as she demonstrates, in some way, a careful reading of the text" (p. 239).

At the heart of both response statements and response essays is the way writing is constructed in the writing-to-learn movement, which, as explained earlier in this chapter, has provided important perspectives from which to develop the notion of writing for reading. As we saw previously, writing in this context is conceptualized as a medium through which students process material they have encountered and their experiences of those encounters. McLeod and Maimon (2000), for instance, speak of writing-to-learn tasks as places where teachers give assignments in which students "use writing as a tool for learning rather than a test of that learning" (p. 579).

This is the essential function that response statements and response essays perform.

Journals

In both the L1 and L2 writing fields, student journal writing has attracted considerable interest. (For especially helpful looks at journal writing in the L1 context, see Fulwiler, 1987; Gardner & Fulwiler, 1999. Particularly helpful in the L2 context are Mlynarczyk, 1998; Peyton, 1990; Peyton & Reed 1990; Peyton & Staton, 1991.) Usually featuring informal and un- or semi-structured writing, journals are attractive to students and teachers because "the personal and exploratory nature style helps them [students] generate interpretive abstractions. Writing really does become an instrument of learning" (Thomson, 1993, p. 142) as students use journals to examine and respond to their reading of other educational experiences. Looking at them specifically from the L2 context, Weissberg (1998) points out that "journal writing replicates for learners many of the benefits of conversational exchange, while at the same time preserving the un-threatening privacy of writing" (p. 3). Lay (1995) discusses their value in developing L2 students' critical-thinking skills and in using writing to interact with reading (pp. 38–39). Looking further at the writing-reading link, Sheridan (1991) says of journal writing that "it is exploratory writing to enhance exploratory reading" (p. 810), and it is here that we begin to see the connection between journal writing and responding. Working in the spirit of Sheridan's model, students can use journal writing to construct response statements, to critically assess their reading, to position themselves for continued reading by making predictions of what is to come in the text or by discussing how they intend to read the remaining portions of the text, and so forth. In each case there is an element of response writing involved—responses to the text or to themselves as readers. Thomson (1993) says of his journal pedagogy that "in their reading journals my students have to tell the story of their reading of texts" (143), and it is in this telling that writing supports reading. Dialogue journals, in which teachers respond actively to students' journal entries and so create a kind of on-going written dialogue, can be especially helpful with respect to writing enhancing reading. As Walworth (1990) observes: "Dialogue journals focus squarely on the learner; learning proceeds in steps beginning from where the learner happens to be rather than from some preconceived model coming from the outside" (p. 46). And, she says, as the teacher engages (through responses) in this written dialogue over texts being read and students' reading experiences or stories, opportunities arise for guiding students "to more effective reading techniques" (p. 37).

Sheridan (1991) posits that "we need assignments that ask students to explore reading" (p. 811), and the personal as well as free-form nature of journal writing is especially conducive to such explorations when students use response-based writing to narrate ongoing stories of the reading of a text. Salvatori (1996) speaks of the need for students to perform, in writing, what she calls "introspective reading" (p. 446), that is, "to practice recursive and self monitoring readings" (p. 449) in which they use writing to move back and forth through portions of texts and through their experiences of texts. Journal writing creates especially valuable opportunities for this "self monitoring" process, making it easier and more meaningful for students to respond to themselves as readers and to their assigned texts. In both their writing of journal entries and their later reading of them, as well as of a teacher's comments on them, students can gain insight into the texts themselves and into their performance as readers. Thus, writing in this expressive mode (as well as in the analytic modes of summarizing and synthesizing) can strengthen students' reading as well as draw students' attention to the various acts that constitute reading. For example, students may come to see or better understand the differences between bottom-up and top-down reading or the value in linking a specific approach to reading to the kind of text being read—for example, reading strategies that best fit the reading of information-based texts such as math or science textbooks or aesthetic texts such as short stories and novels. Reading journals in which writing is used to make sense of and reflect on reading and texts can thus play a vital role in cementing the links between writing and reading.

Major Teaching Scenarios

All of the specific kinds of teaching activities we've reviewed in this chapter can be used in individual assignments of shorter duration, such as having students summarize one particular text they've been asked to read or asking them to write journal entries about, say, a story or poem or article they've been assigned. In many instructional circumstances, these may indeed be the best applications of such activities. However, there are also more involved instructional scenarios in which to use writing in support of reading, and now we'll review two of them. These scenarios could exist at just about any level within the educational system, though they are more likely to occur at the high school and college levels. Each of these scenarios offers rich opportunities for students and teachers to position writing *in service to* reading, especially for students who are struggling as L2 readers.

The Sequential Model

This is an approach in which students engage in a *series* of writing tasks revolving, usually, around the reading of a single text or a few texts on the same topic. The writing tasks are carefully arranged or sequenced so as to increase students' understanding of their reading as they move from one task to another within the sequence. The sequence itself generally moves along a continuum in which some kind of informal written response to the text(s) serves as the starting point and in which a more formal, analytic essay represents the end of the sequence. The notion of a continuum applies to this sequence because equal value is seen in response and analysis (unlike in other writing situations, in which one of these modes of writing is seen as superior to the other).

One major application of the sequence approach is Charles
Bazerman's (1980) *conversational model.* Bazerman uses the
analogy or image of conversation because he sees writing as
an ongoing dialogue between (a) the writer and the text being
read and (b) the writer's dialogue within as she or he writes
and rewrites in response to the text. Explaining that "writing
occurs within the context of previous writing and advances
the total sum of the discourse" (p. 658), Bazerman asks students to complete a series of steps that begins with summarizing and paraphrasing (where there's an emphasis on accuracy in reading and writing), moves on to an informal
response essay (an initial reaction to reading), and culminates
in a formal evaluative essay in which students examine and
comment on their own reading. The "conversation" occurs as
the students continually revisit their earlier reading and writing about the assigned text as they compose new readings and
types of writing involving that text. Here they converse both
with themselves as they explore their own reading activity
and with the teacher as they share what they have found.

Probably the most prominent application of the sequence
approach is the one developed by Donald Bartholomae and
Anthony Petrosky and described in their previously cited
books *Facts, Artifacts, and Counterfacts* (1986) and *Ways of
Reading* (1987). These books discuss—and *Ways of Reading*
serves as a textbook for—an undergraduate writing course
they developed at the University of Pittsburgh. The basis for
that course and the approach it advocates, as well as for similar work that can be done with L2 writers/readers, is located
in the following statement from the resource book they developed for teachers of the course:

> Our students . . . felt powerless in the face of serious writ-
> ing, in the face of long and complicated texts—the kinds of
> texts we thought they should find interesting and chal-
> lenging. We thought (as many teachers of writing have
> thought) that if we just, finally, gave them something good
> to read—something rich and meaty—they would change
> forever their ways of thinking about English. It didn't work,

of course. The issue is not only what students read, but what they can learn to do with what they read. (1996, p. 1)

In their course, then, writing is used partly as a means of making sense of reading. As this takes place in the sequence of writing tasks students must complete, they learn about writing as well as reading. Working on the belief that "a text in our class . . . becomes an occasion for meaning, not a meaning in itself" (1986, p. 14), Bartholomae and Petrosky ask students to read several texts within each of several sequences in a semester-long course and then, during each sequence, to write along a continuum similar to that described earlier for Bazerman's conversational model: "Students follow a sequence of assignments that begins with Bleich's response heuristic and then moves to more critical examination of responses and the assumptions underlying them" (Petrosky, 1982, p. 34). Bartholomae (1986) says that in this approach, reading is conceptualized in such a way that comprehension of a text "is not an act of recognition but something that is initiated by a response justified by the elaboration or extension of that response" (p. 91).

This technique has received some support among L2 writing specialists. Spack (1985, 1988, 1993), for example, has long endorsed the notion of a sequenced approach to academic reading and writing, moving from pre-reading writing to response tasks to analytic essays. As she sees it, "By sequencing assignments, the teacher can move the students away from a primarily personal approach to a more critical approach to the readings" (1988, p. 44). In this way, students can develop useful academic writing skills and use writing to sharpen their reading skills. Zamel (1992) has described an approach in which "we sequence assignments around readings so that students are guided to address these readings from different perspectives" (p. 479), ranging from their own experiences and responses relative to the topic discussed in the text(s) to evaluative essays in which students examine the topic itself and their own earlier writing about the topic.

Blanton, too, has explored the value of sequencing reading and writing. Within this framework, she says, "it is students' continued interaction [through writing] with texts that transforms them into readers, writers, and academically/cognitively proficient people" (1993, p. 238).

ESL teachers can use sequencing in conjunction with texts students must read for other courses or for texts assigned in the ESL course. The complexity and subject matter of these texts could vary according to the educational level and language proficiency of the students. So, too, could the nature of the writing tasks assigned to assist the reading. If, for example, the topic of the text(s) is one the students may have some personal familiarity with, some form of autobiographical writing, especially prior to reading, might provide an effective opening into the text(s) at hand. This would be especially true if students are reading a literary work, such as *The Catcher in the Rye* (where students could reflect on their own experiences of alienation and of frustration in school), or an essay on a contemporary topic touching on students' lives (e.g., the advantages and disadvantages of video games). Reading of a more informational nature, such as a textbook for a history or science or mathematics class, could be supported initially by the summarizing and paraphrasing Bazerman uses in his conversational model. Later, through a task like Salvatori's "difficulty paper" or entries in a reading journal, students could reflect on how they read the text(s). As a final step, they could compose a synthesis essay if more than one text has been assigned. Whether used in a high school or college setting, these scenarios would allow students to use writing as an important tool for reading and would ideally lead to better reading and better writing through the practice and engagement provided during the sequence of assignments.

Content-Based Instruction

Another valuable way of using writing to enhance reading is the content-based approach to teaching and learning in which the writing class (or the ESL class in general) is used as a site for students' explorations of assignments from other courses. Also known, in one formulation, as the *adjunct model,* this approach normally involves a link between an ESL course and a content course, such as, say, a history class. Working in conjunction with the teacher(s) of a content course, the ESL instructor creates opportunities for students to use the ESL class as a place to investigate the reading and writing skills (and perhaps other language skills) necessary in the content course or in academic writing in more general terms. (For helpful, detailed accounts of content-based instruction in the L2 context, see Brinton, Snow, and Wesche, 2003; Kasper, 2000; Snow, 1998; and Snow & Brinton, 1988). Shih (1986) explains what usually occurs in these terms:

> In content-based composition instruction, writing tasks require students to restate and recast information and ideas from readings, lectures, and discussions on a topic and possibly also to report on results of independent group research on related topics. Thus, students develop strategies for collecting, synthesizing, and interpreting new information from external sources as well as for connecting such new information to previous knowledge and skills. (p. 628)

Because so much information in content courses is communicated through course readings, the content-based model becomes an especially attractive option for using writing to support reading. Students can, for instance, be asked to use the summarizing, synthesizing, and response activities to perform the restating and recasting Shih mentions. As students write about the types of texts and the reading difficulties they encounter in a particular content course, teachers can use that writing as a basis for focused discussion of strategies for reading the text types involved and for coping with the reading difficulties students experience. Meanwhile, the students' writing in itself (whether in the form of responses or more analytic writing tasks) can allow them to lend shape to their reading and to see their reading in new and more helpful terms.

Students in K–12 settings, in particular, could be helped significantly by the opportunity to work with an ESL teacher (or in an ESL course) within a content-based framework. The opportunity to use the ESL course, especially writing activities, to learn to read the texts assigned in content courses could provide students with the knowledge, skills, and confidence necessary to perform reading assignments effectively. An ESL teacher could work closely with, say, a biology teacher and use the reading assignments from the biology course as the primary material in the ESL course. Students' written summaries and syntheses of the biology readings could be discussed in the ESL course as a way of drawing attention to students' strengths as readers, addressing their reading problems, discussing effective approaches to such reading, and looking at students' writing as a form of composing similar to that which takes place in reading. Meanwhile, students would be adding to their knowledge of the subject—in this case, biology—and at the same time gradually improving their reading (and writing) skills.

Conclusion

At the heart of this chapter is an attempt to put reading and the struggles L2 students often have with it in a richer context that highlights the act of composing at the heart of reading. Such an act is not a linear one in which students proceed smoothly and in a direct line through a text. Instead, as problems occur with vocabulary, complex grammatical structures, and unfamiliar rhetorical devices, our students are likely to encounter numerous false starts and moments of despair and anxiety as they face texts more difficult than their current L2 proficiency allows them to process fully. While teaching students various reading strategies is helpful, it doesn't, in the end, help them see "reading as dialogic" (Leki, 1993, p. 22), that is, as an ongoing process of interaction between reader and text. Lent (1993) asserts that "we need to provide a place for the working out of reading that goes on during reading" (p.

239), with writing being that place. Kauffman (1996) points out that "through writing about and discussing a text, students will become aware of what they do (and what they don't) know about the text from their reading, and will be able to return to the text with new questions and insights" (pp. 397–398). Writing, then, serves reading and readers in a variety of ways likely to be of particular value to L2 students. Whether used before, during, or after reading, writing enables students to make sense of reading and, just as importantly, makes more visible to them the important connections between reading and writing, thus breaking down the often counterproductive separation between reading and writing that occurs in ESL and EFL classrooms.

The activities and scenarios described in this chapter should help students in different school settings and with varying degrees of language proficiency learn to approach L2 reading with greater understanding as they summarize, synthesize, and/or respond to texts. L2 reading, especially when it involves the complex texts often assigned in high school and college, can be a lonely and exasperating, if not crippling, experience for many of our students. The types of composing that writing as discussed in this chapter involves helps students because it "slows down thought processes, inviting considerations of ideas and questions" (Faust, 2000, p. 17), and removes from reading the sometimes solitary nature that seems to deter many students. Petrosky (1982) tells us that "writing about reading is one of the best ways to get students to unravel their transactions" (p. 24). As they do so, both students (as they write and read their responses or summaries or syntheses) and teachers (as we read and analyze their writing about their reading) acquire new and valuable information about L2 students as readers and about L2 reading itself.

As teachers, we need, of course, to provide students with the kind of support that allows them to understand reading as well as to become better at it. As we increase our own understanding of reading-writing connections, it is imperative that we bear in mind this view of writing as serving reading.

Questions for Reflection and Discussion

1. To what extent and in what ways have you used writing-to-read/writing-for-reading strategies in your L1 and/or your L2?
2. Of Eisterhold's three models of reading-writing connections discussed at the beginning of this chapter—directional, nondirectional, and bidirectional—which do you find most appealing as a writer/reader and relative to your current or anticipated teaching context? Why?
3. What's your reaction to Leki's criticisms of reading instruction? Why?
4. Discuss your responses to Zamel's previously cited comment that "writing is the foundation of reading; it may be the most basic way to learn about reading"? Does her observation match your own experience as a learner and/or teacher? Why?
5. Summarizing, one of the primary writing-to-read strategies, seems to be especially difficult for many L2 writers/readers. What, in your view, are the causes of these difficulties? And what, in your view or experience, are some of the most effective means for helping students learn to summarize effectively in their L2?
6. Of the two major *objective* writing-for-reading strategies discussed in this chapter—summarizing and synthesizing—which, in your view, is likely to be more effective for your students as a means of linking writing and reading? Why?
7. What's your response to Salvatori's "difficulty paper" idea? Would this work well with your own students? Why or why not?

Chapter 4

Reading to Write

Because this chapter is so closely connected to Chapter 3, let's briefly review a few key points from that chapter that provide a helpful lead-in to this chapter.

First, reading-writing relations can be approached from three models: directional, nondirectional, and bidirectional (Eisterhold 1990). The directional model, which Eisterhold saw as the most salient model from the teaching perspective, is the one underpinning Chapters 3 and 4. While acknowledging the intricate connections and reciprocity between reading and writing, the directional model nevertheless works on the premise of a primary movement from writing to reading or from reading to writing.

In Chapter 3, we saw the "from writing to reading" movement in terms of writing supporting reading, and within that, this dominant theme: that writing serves as an invaluable tool in *allowing readers to make sense of reading.* Writing about reading strengthens reading.

In this chapter, we'll see reading-writing connections cast in a somewhat different light than in Chapter 3. Here, we'll look principally at the role of *input* in connecting reading and writing. More specifically, we'll explore how various uses of target language input deriving from reading influence writing development. The theme of this chapter is that it's primarily through meaningful input that reading supports writing.

Various terms are used when discussing the core notion of *from reading to writing.* These include *reading for writing, reading to write, reading while writing,* and *writerly reading.* In essence, they are all related to the fundamental belief that at least in academic or school settings, *reading is a prelude to writing that shapes writing.* Carson (1993) provides a nice definition of this notion:

> The phrase *reading for writing* can be understood as referring most specifically to the literacy event in which readers/writers use text(s) that they read, or have read, as a basis for text(s) that they write. . . . Reading for writing can also be understood as acknowledging that writing is often the resultant physical artifact of reading/writing encounters. (p. 85)

To flesh this definition out a little more, consider these few well-known statements that, in general terms, frame discussions of *reading for writing* (the term to be used in the remainder of this chapter):

> Probably no one doubts that reading plays a major role in learning to write. (Bereiter & Scardamalia, 1984, p. 163).

> . . . reading is what makes it possible for us to write rather than the other way around. (Leki, 1992, p. 468)

> Teaching writing without teaching reading is not teaching writing at all. (Kroll, 1993, p. 75)

> Everything points to the necessity of learning to write from what we read. (Smith, 1983, p. 560)

In this chapter, we'll explore the basis for such statements and discuss their implications for and applications in classroom practice. Before looking at some of the specific ways in which writing for reading is categorized and discussed, let's first provide more of the framework for looking at reading-writing connections from this direction.

In his often cited book *Writing: Research, Theory, and Applications* (1984), Stephen Krashen links the well-known distinction between competence and performance—a distinction at the heart of the dominant communicative language teaching methodology—to the acquisition of writing skills. We know that *competence* refers to knowledge of something, while *performance* refers to the ability to use the knowledge stored in competence. With respect to writing, Krashen explains:

> We gain competence in writing the same way we gain competence in oral language: by understanding messages encoded in written language, by reading for meaning. In this way we gain a subconscious "feel" for written language, we acquire this code as a second dialect. (pp. 27–28)

This statement is at the heart of Krashen's belief that "it is reading that gives the writer the 'feel' for the look and texture of reader-based prose" (p. 20). Krashen goes on to say that

> The competence/performance theory . . . implies that instruction in writing should not focus on teaching form directly, but should instead encourage the subconscious acquisition of form through reading and give students procedures that will facilitate the discovery of meaning and an efficient writing process. (p. 39)

In other words, knowledge of writing comes from the input provided by reading. In this case, Krashen's use of the term *form* refers to the rules or conventions of writing in the target language. Because these rules and conventions, which may vary considerably from those guiding writing in the students' native language, are often difficult for students to learn directly through explicit instruction in them, we may be better served in the writing classroom by providing reading materials and activities that allow learners meaningful exposure to writing in the target language. Through this exposure and the natural processes at the heart of acquisition (as opposed to conscious learning), learners are better able to internalize L2 writing rules and conventions, thus putting in place the competence they must draw from while attempting to write in the target language. Effective performance in L2 writing is less

likely to occur if appropriate competence has not been established. The role of reading is to provide the grounds for that
competence. As Leki (1993) notes, "We know that reading
builds knowledge of various kinds to use in writing" (p. 10).
And so, as Carson and Leki (1993a) point out, "reading can
be, and in academic settings nearly always is, the basis for
writing" (p. 1). This is not just because it is the nature of academic life in high school and college to write about material
one has read; it's also because of the valuable *input* about writing provided by reading. Thus, reading-for-writing work revolves around two key questions: *what kind of input should
teachers provide students, and in what form should that input appear and be treated?* This chapter is primarily an attempt to share helpful answers to those questions.

In considering reading for writing, then, we need to extend
our notion of reading, particularly in our writing classrooms.
Instead of assigning texts because of the information about a
subject they can provide writers, we can also take into account the texts' value as sources of knowledge or input about
writing itself. Ideally, we'll want our developing L2 writers to
learn about writing itself—not just the subject at hand—
through what they read. Thus, say Bloch and Chi (1995),
"Reading in the composition class need not be simply about
learning facts but about how writers think through the problems they are addressing" (p. 271). Kroll (1993) makes a similar point while noting that "one can read a text not only to
'learn' its content but to 'learn' choices that writers have made
in producing it" (p. 72). Whether by the act of reading itself
or through learning by instruction, students can, for example,
acquire knowledge about L2 writing by looking at the rhetorical decisions made by authors, that is, why certain information was arranged as it was by the author (i.e., rhetorical reading). Understanding this kind of organizational information
allows readers to gain insight into the principles of construction of target language writing, such as where to locate thesis
statements, topic sentences, examples and other supporting
material, and so forth. This kind of reading is also valuable in
an area like learning how the words and ideas of others are in-

tegrated into one's writing. Stotsky (1995) summarizes the benefits accruing from using reading input for writing development when she observes that "reading experience would seem to be the chief source of a developing writer's syntactic, generic, and lexical knowledge" (p. 773).

What we will see in this chapter, then, is, as Selfe (1986) describes it, "reading as a productive writing strategy" (p. 46), in which reading is presented to students as a means of learning about the components that constitute writing and/or as a way of experiencing the meaning-making that, as we saw in earlier chapters, is common to both reading and writing. This means, according to Zamel (1992), helping students recognize "that reading is a process of composing" (p. 480).

Berthoff (1983) asserts that "how we construe is how we construct" (p. 167) with respect to reading and writing. If students are to write effectively (construct), they must have reading experiences through which they acquire valuable information and understanding about the elements that constitute writing (construe).

In this chapter, we examine this notion in greater detail. In the process, we establish a framework by which to follow the advice of Tierney and Leys (1986), who say that when we teach reading, we can "treat our readers as if they were writers" (p. 19). How and why we can do that will be the focus of the remainder of this chapter.

We first take a closer look at the role of input in reading-for-writing work and then examine two primary models from which to view reading for writing: a *direct model,* in which students are shown, explicitly, how to approach reading from a writer's perspective in order to gain access to information about writing; and an *indirect model,* in which readers learn about writing less overtly through the types of reading they engage in. Here is where we see an application of the learning-acquisition distinction, in that the direct model encourages conscious learning about writing through reading, while the indirect model works from the belief that students will acquire, naturally, in the course of reading, knowledge of and information about writing; that is, they will acquire such knowledge and information through meaningful exposure to writing in the form of reading.

The Direct Model of Reading for Writing

At the heart of this model of reading for writing is the belief that learners learn best when they seek consciously for information and understanding. In this case, of course, we mean actively seeking to learn about writing through reading. Indeed, the sole or main purpose for reading will be to obtain knowledge about writing. This can mean learning about common *rhetorical* or *organizational* patterns in target language writing (e.g., location of such staples of writing in English as thesis statements and topic sentences), studying *linguistic* features of writing (e.g., transitional words and phrases, the frequency of certain verb tenses in specific kinds of situations), and examining *lexical* as well as *stylistic* characteristics of writing (e.g., the use of informal and formal vocabulary in different circumstances). Before looking at common applications of this model, we briefly review two particularly interesting ways of viewing the direct act of reading for writing: *mining* and *writerly reading.*

Mining

This analogy for describing the process of reading with the intention of learning about writing is meant to conjure up the image of miners digging out coal or some other valuable resource. Between looking for sources of the material they're seeking and then physically extracting that material, miners operate with a clear and direct purpose in mind. In the same way, learners using reading to gain knowledge about writing act as miners exploring their source texts for the input being sought. In the classroom setting under the guidance of a teacher, the kinds of knowledge students look for may be identified ahead of time, perhaps using the labels mentioned earlier—rhetorical, linguistic, or lexical input.

Stuart Greene, a prominent advocate of mining, explains it this way:

> Whereas teachers often encourage a critical reading of individual texts as an end in itself, mining is part of an ongoing effort to learn specific rhetorical and linguistic conventions. The strategies students observe in reading can become part of their own repertoire for writing on different occasions. (1993, p. 36)

In this "mindful study of texts" (Greene, 1993, p. 35), readers are not only conducting a search for valuable input about writing; they are also adopting a certain stance toward the act of reading. To continue with Greene's (1993) perspectives on mining, students move from what many writers have referred to as the "spectator role," in which they passively decode what is in the text being read, to a "participant's role," in which they actively engage the text (somewhat in the vein of the reader-response approach discussed in Chapter 2).

By conceptualizing and presenting reading in this way to students and by casting them in the participant's role, in which mining is their key activity, teachers can achieve two important goals in the domain of reading-writing connections: (1) moving L2 students away from the more passive approach to reading that many may adopt to one in which reading, by its active and participatory nature, becomes more interesting or useful than it might otherwise be for many students; and (2) ensuring that students make contact with the elements of L2 writing they need exposure to in order to bring those elements into their own writing repertoires. By carefully selecting the texts students read and offering guidance in terms of what they can or should look for, teachers are in a position to ensure that students gain meaningful exposure to the properties of target language writing that students need to command. Furthermore, through this directive approach to these properties of writing, students are better positioned to learn, not just make superficial contact with, this crucial information about writing. Accompanying reading and writing

tasks that aim to reinforce students' knowledge and understanding of these writing features strengthen the direct model.

The kind of mining for information about writing just described does not have to occur only through the directive
guidance of a teacher. Learners can also conduct their mining
operations on their own using texts of their own choice. They
might, for example, have favorite subjects they read about in
magazines or via websites, such as music or fashions, and
they can simultaneously read for information about the subject itself as well as about target language writing.

With respect to "mining," then, students are active explor-
ers of texts, sometimes knowing what kinds of features they're
looking for and sometimes knowing only that they wish to use
reading to learn about writing. Whether we as teachers choose
to draw our students' attention to this mining analogy or simply use it ourselves as a guiding image in designing our reading for writing tasks, the concept of mining is a particularly
appealing and helpful one in characterizing what it means to
engage in reading for writing. A related analogy I've used in
my own classes with some success is that of detectives; that
is, students are asked to place themselves in the role of detectives in search of important clues about L2 writing as they
read the texts I assign. By "clues" I mean rhetorical or linguistic features in texts that enable them to succeed as texts.

Teaching suggestion: Adventurous teachers, particularly
in school (as opposed to college) settings, can arrange for
students to actually dress as miners or detectives by supplying materials of the kind miners and detectives use:
helmets, flashlights, magnifying glasses, and so forth.
Once dressed in this way, students can then work in pairs
or groups or individually, conducting their searches for
the features or clues in writing the teacher wishes them
to learn more about. This activity can even be conducted
in a kind of game format in which students compete to
find clues. For example, they can be asked to find words

and phrases that serve as cohesive devices in texts, that is, linking sentences and/or paragraphs together. Supplying students with the paraphernalia of mining or detective work can reinforce the point that this is the nature of what they can do as readers/writers.

Writerly Reading

As with the "mining" concept, the notion of writerly reading is based on the idea of highly directed or directive reading in which readers consciously attempt to learn about writing from reading. Indeed, Greene (1993) sees this as a type of mining activity, and the two types of writing do overlap. Both are united by Donald Murray's (1982) term "reading writer." Murray describes the action of the reading writer as follows: "The reading writer—the map-maker and map-reader—reads the word, the line, the sentence, the paragraph, the page, the entire text. This constant back-and-forth reading monitors the multiple complex relationships between all the elements in writing" (p. 142). Where the separation occurs is in the role or stance adopted by the reader. As we saw with mining, the reader takes on the persona of a miner or detective hunting for clues about writing, but the writerly reader takes on the persona of the writer of the text being read; that is, "To read like a writer we engage with the author in what the author is writing. We anticipate what the author will say, so that the author is in effect writing on our behalf, not showing how something is done but doing it with us" (Smith, 1983, p. 563). For example, the writerly reader is constantly making predictions about what comes next in a text by trying to think as the writer of the text must have been thinking at various points in the development of the text. Through this process of in essence being the writer, the reader gains greater sensitivity to and understanding of what happens during writing. This, clearly, is not reading for comprehension of content; the purpose is, by thinking like a writer rather than a reader, to focus on and better understand the features of writing that make the text work as a piece of writing.

This conceptualization of reading mirrors two of the best-known descriptions of reading: Smith's (1971) notion of reading as a process of "hypothesis testing" and Goodman's (1968) characterization of reading as a "psycholinguistic guessing game." However, those statements still position the reader as someone reading another person's text and for the purpose of comprehension. To understand writerly reading, we need to see the reader as continually trying to *be* the writer. The reader is thus asking such questions as "If I were writing this, what sentence would come next?" or "What transitional word or phrase would I use here to link the previous passage and the next one?" In trying to form answers to these questions and then seeing how the writer of the text actually proceeded, the reader is continually seeking to acquire knowledge of the specific features of writing by experiencing the decision-making process that constitutes writing. Writers make decisions constantly about the words they'll use, where they'll put them, which information to include in the text, and so forth. Since these decisions in a foreign language may be very different from those made by writers in students' L1, it's especially important for them to enter the decision-making process of target language writers. While they of course can practice that process directly through their own target language writing, they first need an awareness of the linguistic and rhetorical tools at their disposal while they write. That's what writerly reading does. By constructing reading as an activity in which the reader basically pretends to be a writer, greater attention is paid to the features and operations of writing. This is, as we have seen elsewhere in this book, a variation of the core notion of reading as *composing* (as opposed to decoding the meaning of a text), that is, reading as an act of construction. What's being constructed in this case is the acts of writing that make the text what it is. Hunt (1985) describes the writerly reading activity this way:

> They read a text, a paragraph, a sentence, a word, as if they were writing it, using the structure they are building in their minds, and their knowledge of the codes of writing within which the text is being constructed. These serve as devices to anticipate what might be coming next to reor-

ganize what they have already read, both in the short and the long term. Thus, the reader's attention is predominantly constructive: they look not at things, but at possible relations between things. (pp. 162–163)

When readers read in this way, says Smith (1983), "Bit by bit, one thing at a time, but enormous things over the passage of time, the learner learns through *reading* like a writer to *write* like a writer" (p. 564).

Teaching suggestion: Many teachers will already be familiar with the venerable "jigsaw puzzle" teaching strategy in which a teacher takes a text and cuts it into pieces. Students are given the pieces and then asked to assemble them into a coherent text. This technique is especially applicable from the writerly reading perspective. However, from this perspective, it would be important to ask students to think consciously like the writer of the text as they assemble the pieces of the text.

The jigsaw might be presented differently. For instance, students might be given the first part of the text intact so as to provide a launching point from which to view the text as a writer. Also, there could be considerably more cutting up of the text so that students would have to make more "writerly" decisions in the reassembly of the text at various levels (word, sentence, paragraph). In addition, students might be asked to compose their own pieces—at the sentence or paragraph level—to provide linkage between pieces. While this would be a considerably challenging exercise, in deciding how to create a bridge in writing between two already written pieces of the text, they would have to give even more careful thought to how the writer must have been thinking at that point. This would heighten their awareness of features of target language writing as they sift through the linguistic and rhetorical decisions necessary to create this "missing link" of the text.

To sum up, writerly reading is the act of thinking like a *writer* while reading. For many students, this would be a challenging role to assume, and careful framing of it in the classroom would likely be necessary. However, as another technique for learning directly about writing through reading, it reinforces the notion of *close reading* of texts in order to extract writerly information from them. Furthermore, this type of reading activity may make the act of target language reading more meaningful for students; that is, they will recognize that concrete benefits will accrue from their reading, and this can better motivate reading than can merely reading for comprehension. The bottom line is that "to the extent that students learn to read in this way, they also tend to learn to write better from their reading" (Hunt, 1985, p. 163).

Rhetorical Reading

The notions of mining and writerly reading have offered some macro-level ways of looking at the use of reading to learn about writing; that is, they've illustrated, in general terms, processes by which students can approach reading within an integrated reading-writing framework. Now we can turn our attention to specific, or micro-level, ways of applying the concepts of mining and writerly reading.

One of those ways, an approach that has been discussed in ESL/EFL terms since the early 1980s, is *rhetorical reading.* This application of mining and, especially, writerly reading takes two primary forms. One is an explicit approach in which students are first taught about the primary rhetorical features of texts in the target language and then asked to use that knowledge in their own reading of such texts. Research into the effectiveness of this approach, as Carrell and Connor (1991) note, "suggest[s] that explicit training in rhetorical structures for ESL reading facilitates ESL writing" (p. 314); that is, students are encouraged to use what they know about the organization of L2 texts not just to empower their reading but to inform their writing as well. Here, reinforcement in the form of writing assignments following rhetorical reading assignments is especially important. For instance, students can be taught about elements of writing like the transitional words and phrases that signal shifts in focus and can then be asked to locate them in texts they've been asked to read—for example, by underlining or in some other way identifying those features. Follow-up writing assignments can require that they include the same features in their own essays. Given the rhetorical differences that exist between English and many other languages, as demonstrated by research in contrastive rhetoric, directing students' attention to primary and secondary rhetorical features of L2 texts is a natural approach to follow in equipping students to use the target language as readers and writers.

Another pedagogical approach to rhetorical reading is to help students analyze and learn from the "rhetorical situation" in which a text has been written. This approach has been especially popular in the teaching of English as an L1, particularly in the work of Haas and Flower in the 1980s, but it has value in the L2 context as well. The main idea in this approach is first to look closely at the situation motivating the writer to produce her or his text and then to study the strategies adopted by the writer to generate a text that addresses the rhetorical situation at hand. Here's how Haas and Flower (1988) describe the approach:

> *Rhetorical strategies* take a step beyond the text itself. They are concerned with constructing a rhetorical situation for the text, trying to account for an author's purpose, context, and effect on the audience. In rhetorical reading strategies, readers use cues in the text, and their own knowledge of discourse situations, to recreate or infer the rhetorical situation of the text they are reading. (p. 176)

Here's an example of a rhetorical situation. Take the controversial topic of bilingual education (an excellent topic to use with high school and college ESL students in a North American setting, because of the relevant linguistic and cultural issues it raises). An author writing, say, a persuasive essay for or against bilingual education has as her rhetorical situation the need to organize and present evidence in support of her position. She will have to make numerous decisions in terms of how to organize the essay as a whole and where to place specific pieces of information within the essay so as to convince the audience to adopt her point of view. Thus, the writing decisions she makes and the rhetorical elements that make up her text will be responses to that persuasively or argumentatively based rhetorical situation. This is the situation students would analyze in the process of conducting a rhetorical reading of her text. Knowing of her stance on the issue, they could then analyze the text to see how she arranged it to support the rhetorical situation of arguing in favor of her position on bilingual education.

Here again, reading is conceived of as more than an act of comprehension of meaning. Instead, and consistent with the notions of mining and writerly reading, students are asked to take an approach to reading in which they try to produce knowledge of writing. This is not a passive view of reading or the teaching of reading. It is a productive act. As Haas and Flower (1988) explain, "Seeing reading as a constructive act encourages us as teachers to move from merely *teaching texts* to *teaching readers*" (p. 169). In other words, we are not merely teaching students what, rhetorically, is in L2 texts, but we are passing along a message about how they can interact with texts while they read them. Instead of merely teaching mechanical techniques for reading, we are imagining students *engaged in* the act of reading. And, just as importantly, we are linking reading to writing through an emphasis on how the knowledge of writing gained through rhetorical reading can be applied in writing. In the case of the approach to rhetorical reading advocated by Haas and Flower (among others), the idea is to help students learn to write by using their understanding of an author's rhetorical intentions and expectations to guide their reading of a text and, thus, to acquire knowledge of writing.

In explicating this approach to rhetorical reading, Haas and Flower work with a distinction that has been of great significance in the teaching of L1 (and L2) writing in English: that between what they call "knowledge getting" and "knowledge telling" (or "knowledge transforming"). *Knowledge getting* is basically the act of obtaining knowledge or information from reading, while *knowledge telling* is using that input from reading while writing. An underlying concern in their construction of this distinction is that too often teachers separate the acts of knowledge getting and telling by conveying to students the notion that knowledge getting applies solely to reading and knowledge telling applies only to writing. In their view, "Helping students move beyond this simple information-exchange view to a more complex rhetorical model—in both their reading and writing—is one of the very real tasks which faces us as teachers" (p. 182). Their belief is that teaching students how to analyze rhetorical *situations,* not just texts themselves, promotes a link between knowledge getting and knowledge telling, in that students will carry into their reading an underlying purpose of wanting to use the knowledge of writing they gain through their reading. By reading for a *rhetorical purpose,* rather than strictly for comprehension of meaning, a knowledge-telling function is embedded within the knowledge getting that will drive students' reading.

This dichotomy between knowledge getting and telling, as well as the attempt to use it more constructively through an inclusive view that links the two acts through rhetorically based reading/writing instruction, is of particular significance in L2 reading and writing, where students may well see reading purely as knowledge getting (and only for acquiring knowledge of the topic they're reading and perhaps writing about). Indeed, that may be the only way in which they were encouraged to view L2 reading in prior instruction. If an accompanying notion of knowledge telling is linked to their reading, a notion by which they will be looking, as they read, for ways to use their knowledge of writing gained through reading, their reading will take on an entirely new meaning. Studying the *rhetorical situation* in which the text is located will draw students' attention to the writerly decisions the author made in producing the text being read. Understanding those decisions as they read the text is not only knowledge getting, *if they have been encouraged to read for writing purposes;* it is also knowledge telling or the basis for that telling, because students carry into their reading an expectation that they will use that knowledge in their writing.

Whichever approach to rhetorical reading is adopted by teachers, the bottom line, says Kroll (1993), is that "writing teachers need to understand how to train their students in reading a text rhetorically, because this is a process that promotes the integration of reading and writing" (pp. 71–72). Indeed, rhetorical reading transforms the act of reading by foregrounding the use of reading to gain knowledge of writing. Working as miners or writerly readers as they engage the rhetorical features of L2 texts, students will be stockpiling information about L2 writing that will expand their repertoire of L2 writing strategies to draw from while writing.

Teaching suggestion: Students can be assigned a topic to read and write about—school uniforms, for example. They can be asked to read a variety of texts on this topic: some that simply provide background information about the topic, some that argue for or against school uniforms, and some that aim to provide a look at both sides of the issue without taking sides. Prior to their reading of these texts, they can be given information about the kinds of rhetorical strategies most often used by writers of such text types. Their task then becomes to locate those rhetorical strategies in the texts and—working in pairs, groups, or individually—report to the class orally or to the teacher in some written form what they have found. This mining work might include comparing the rhetorical strategies of the writers involved, such as those arguing in support of and opposition to school uniforms. They can also report on why they think the authors used particular strategies (analysis of rhetorical situation). As a follow-up writing activity linked to this reading, they can write their own essay on school uniforms using the rhetorical information gathered through their reading. To ensure the the linking of *knowledge getting* and *knowledge telling*, students can be told before they begin their reading that they will have to use the input about writing they locate while *mining* rhetorically. In this way the process of knowledge getting is already shifting to knowledge telling, because students will begin to anticipate, while reading, how they will apply that knowledge in writing.

The Modeling Approach

This direct approach to using reading for learning about writing is probably the one most familiar to teachers, either through their own experiences as students or in their practice as language teachers. The idea is simple: have students study, through close reading, models of the kinds of texts they're expected to write. There is nothing new in this approach. In fact, as Smagorinsky (1992) observes, "The practice of reading model essays to learn writing skills can be traced to antiquity" (p. 161). And, unlike the earlier direct approaches we reviewed, this one is most suited to working with students at all school levels, including children in elementary school language classes. That's because students from elementary school through graduate school all deal, as readers and writers, with *genres,* or types of writing, of some kind. For elementary school students, it might be writing poems, stories, diaries or journals, or short informative reports. Middle and high school students may face such common tasks as writing book reports, responses to literary (or non-literary) texts, lab reports in science classes, journals, summaries, argumentative essays, and so forth. The same kinds of assignments could be found at the college level, though with more complex expectations. Graduate students will encounter such tasks as writing literature reviews and critical reviews, journal articles for publication, conference papers, and theses and dissertations.

Whichever school context they're in, students writing in a second or foreign language will probably want and benefit from models of the text types they're writing, particularly since these text types might be completely unfamiliar to them. This very desire on their part carries with it an implied valuing of the notion of using reading for writing purposes, since the use of models begins with the reading of them. The template or blueprint they hope to imitate must first be analyzed in the act of reading through the approaches and notions we've already discussed. In processing model texts as readers, students step into the roles of miners or writerly readers and engage in specific acts of rhetorical reading. In doing so, they intuitively understand or sense that they can apply what they observe through their reading. Teachers have that same intuition. Thus, "Reading has played an important role in the writing classroom because we believe that students can learn about writing through imitating models of well wrought prose. The expectation is that students will internalize the style, grace, and correctness that make these works exemplary" (Greene, 1993, p. 34).

What we can do as teachers is to guide the process in ways that allow students to make the best possible uses of this type of reading. By introducing and working with the notion of rhetorical reading, for example, we can equip students with the tools they need to analyze and learn from the model texts we supply. And in the second language context, if we teach students who have already established L1 reading and writing skills, we can help them utilize the knowledge embedded in those skills as they read the model texts; that is, we can empower them by helping them recognize that they are not entering powerlessly the reading and writing side of imitating models. Conversely, we need to exercise caution when introducing models, as students already able to read and write in a language may unintentionally misuse that knowledge while analyzing target language models. As Bereiter and Scardamalia (1984), writing in the context of native language readers/ writers, point out:

> one of the things that must be taken into account in considering learning about writing from reading is that people

hardly ever start from zero in acquiring a new literary form or convention. They already have some discourse schema to apply, and successful learning from a model must entail either modifying that schema or altering its range of application. (p. 176)

This is a primary reason why there have long been objections to the use of models in writing instruction. In the second language context, in particular, confusion may result from students juxtaposing their native language schema about written texts against what they're learning from target language models. For instance, argumentative writing is very culture bound, with notions of acceptable argumentation varying widely. Interference from the L1 schema might prevent effective use of the L2 rhetorical and linguistic knowledge gained from reading and analyzing texts in the target language.

Still, models expose language learners to target language conventions and practices that they otherwise might have a difficult time understanding. Furthermore, models, like the other approaches to direct use of reading for writing, have the advantage of supplying meaning to L2 reading by injecting added value to the reading. Students who know they will have to produce, in writing, a particular kind of text will likely see reading—that is, mining—model texts as an experience of considerable practical value. And so the use of the modeling approach is especially promising in terms of planting in students a sense of the value of connecting reading and writing and in showing them how the connections actually operate.

The Indirect Model of Reading for Writing

As the name of this model suggests, students reading for writing in this way are not conducting a direct or overt search for input related to writing. Acquiring this input might not be the primary goal for their reading, as comprehension of the source text(s) is naturally a principal concern; it can, however, be a factor motivating the kind of reading we'll be discussing in this section. However, in this approach to reading for writing, unlike the direct model, knowledge of writing is seen more as a natural outcome of reading; that is, exposure, through reading, to writing in the target language will enable students to gain an awareness of how the target language writing operates. Here's where we see the other side of the learning-acquisition distinction. The direct model works on the belief that students will learn more about writing if they intentionally set out to discover things about writing through reading. Knowledge of writing is thus gained consciously and deliberately. By contrast, the indirect model works on a belief in the processes of language *acquisition,* whereby learning occurs on its own when students are presented with what Krashen (1984) calls *comprehensible input.* Within this framework of reading for writing, the input itself and the conditions under which students encounter it take precedence over what students actually do with the input, unlike in the case of a directive strategy like rhetorical reading, where students have a conscious task to perform.

According to Krashen, "Just as comprehensible input is necessary for second language acquisition, but is not sufficient, reading is necessary for acquisition of writing competence" (p. 25). In part, this point of view suggests that writing instruction focusing strictly on writing will have a limited effect, as writing will be seen out of context to some extent without some emphasis on the knowledge of writing that reading provides. In that sense, Krashen reinforces the general notion of reading-writing connections, with input from one skill (reading) helping shape the development of the other (writing). More specifically, though, Krashen is pointing the way to his influential "reading input hypothesis" (1993), in which he asserts that significant amounts of what he calls "self-directed" reading—that is, voluntary reading—by students leads to acquisition of L2 writing ability because of the exposure to target language writing operations such reading provides. *Voluntary reading* as used by Krashen is another term for extensive reading, in which students are encouraged to read widely rather than concentrating on a few texts.

As Eskey and Grabe (1988) have explained, extensive reading is valuable in terms of allowing students ample opportunities to develop the interactive reading strategy (i.e., combination of bottom-up and top-down techniques) and other strategies essential to good reading. Because extensive reading envelops learners in the written form of the target language, it enhances the instantiation of necessary reading skill as students negotiate the texts they encounter. Because this notion is so important in the context of the indirect model of reading for writing, it's worth looking at a longer statement from Krashen (1984) on this issue:

> If second language acquisition and the development of writing ability occur in the same way, writing ability is not learned but is acquired via extensive reading in which the focus of the reader is on the message, i.e., reading for genuine interest and/or for pleasure. Just as speech is hypothesized to be a result of comprehensible input, the ability to write is hypothesized to be the result of reading. Moreover, when enough reading is done, all the necessary grammatical structures and discourse rules for writing will automatically be presented to the writer in sufficient quantity. (p. 23)

Reading, then, provides essential input for writing in both linguistic and rhetorical terms. However, this is not just any type of reading. In the preceding quote from Krashen, a few key terms stand out and need to be explored further: "extensive reading," "reading for genuine interest," and "reading for pleasure." As we'll see in a moment, these kinds of reading differ markedly from the reading that occurs in the direct model of reading for writing. What's notable right away is the emphasis on students reading because they *want* to read, because something about the reading genuinely attracts their interest. That interest provides the meaningful interaction with the text that enables students to consciously or unconsciously acquire information about writing.

There are two primary and overlapping frameworks in which this can occur: extensive reading and free or voluntary reading. Both operate on the principle that reading must be seen by students to be pleasurable; where they differ is in how students encounter the reading material and what they do with it.

Extensive Reading

Extensive reading is partly in contrast to *intensive,* or close, reading of texts. Intensive reading schemes or approaches require students to focus intently on a particular text so as to consciously extract as much useful input from it as possible. This is the kind of reading more likely to occur in the direct model of reading for writing discussed earlier.

Extensive reading schemes take a very different approach. In a typical extensive reading school setting, for example, a particular classroom may serve as a kind of library for students. Here, there will ideally be large quantities of books on a variety of topics and of different genres. Students go there either on their own time or during a designated reading period and look through the collection of books. The key is that *they* decide what they'll read, as opposed to having the teacher assign a text. If the main purpose of this activity is to promote reading ability, students may be asked to record information about their reading, perhaps by filling out index cards whenever they finish and return a book. The cards may simply indicate the title of the book read, the date of its reading, and the name of the student who read it. More ambitious extensive reading schemes may require students to include on the card a short written summary of the book they read.

Because of the fact that they're choosing not only the texts but the subjects they read about, students can then approach this reading from the perspective of "genuine interest" or "pleasure." While the general task of reading is still assigned by the teacher, students take control of the experience and thus read from interest. Extensive reading is based on the core idea of students reading widely, with quantity of texts read an important variable. In a review of the literature on extensive reading, Ferris and Hedgcock (1998) note that "a growing body of evidence suggests that extensive reading—most notably, reading of a voluntary nature—may dramatically enhance the development of linguistic skills, especially those related to comprehending and producing written text" (p. 23).

In another look at the extensive reading literature, Cumming (1989) observes that "extensive reading and other purposeful uses of a second language appear necessary to facilitate the long-term development of effective writing performance" (p. 126). Tsang (1996), for example, found in a study of secondary school students in Hong Kong that an extensive reading scheme "improved general knowledge and thus helped develop content in writing. It also exposed students to appropriate models of construction, agreement, tense, number, and word order/function, which strengthened their use of the language" (p. 228).

A particularly striking example of the application and benefits of extensive reading is found in a study by Elley (1991), who examined the use of extensive reading schemes in schools in a number of South Pacific and Southeast Asian countries. These were schemes in which young children in ESL classrooms were exposed to what were then called "book floods," that is, large quantities of books supplied in the manner described earlier. Elley found that in each case, the extensive reading scheme contributed to development of L2 ability. What's also important, according to Elley, is that the schemes "occur in pleasant, nonthreatening contexts, with associated gains in attitudes toward reading and books" (p. 408). These are the kinds of conditions that Krashen and other advocates of the indirect approach to learning about writing from reading see as particular advantages of this type of reading for writing: an environment that allows students to experience reading more naturally than in the case of the direct approach may be more likely to allow students to acquire meaningful knowledge about writing. (See Day and Bamford, 1998, for a comprehensive treatment of extensive reading.)

Free/Voluntary Reading

This application of the indirect model overlaps significantly with extensive reading. As with extensive reading, the core idea is that learners benefit most from significant amounts of reading in the target language. Where they differ is in how this reading takes place. As the term *free/voluntary reading* suggests, students are left more to their own devices than in extensive reading schemes; that is, the reading occurs outside school, unlike extensive reading (where students may choose their own reading materials according to their own interests but where there is an ostensible structure to the experience by virtue of the schemes often taking place in classroom settings and of students keeping records of their reading). By contrast, with free/voluntary reading students usually engage in reading outside the classroom and under less structured conditions than in extensive reading, though the classroom can be a starting point for such reading (Dupuy, Tse, & Cook, 1996). What is crucial in this approach is what Krashen has called "the pleasure principle." Kim and Krashen (1997) point out:

> It has been established that reading, especially free voluntary reading, is a powerful means of developing second language competence. Those who read more have larger vocabularies, do better on tests of grammar, write better, and spell better. There is also suggestive evidence that extensive pleasure reading can contribute to oral/aural competence as well. (p. 26)

Kim and Krashen (1997) also cite earlier studies by Cho and Krashen (1994, 1995a, 1995b) in which students struggling with English found a way into the language by reading what they called "light reading materials," such as a series of novels called the Sweet Valley High series, and simplified versions of classic novels like Jane Austen's *Emma.* As these books captured students' interest and activated "the pleasure principle," their attitude toward English language learning was transformed into a more positive and confident one. A study by Constantino, Lee, Cho, and Krashen (1997) reported similar reactions. A much cited study of particular relevance to the notion of learning about writing from reading is authored by Janopoulos (1986), who reported gains in the writing of college-level ESL students who engaged in voluntary pleasure reading. The reading material itself—often literary texts in extensive reading schemes and free, voluntary reading—and the positive atmosphere toward learning created by the voluntary nature of the reading experience together are believed to allow students to subconsciously internalize valuable information about writing in the target language.

It is important to note that not all studies of such reading have found positive effects on writing. Hedgcock and Atkinson (1993) and Flahive and Bailey (1993) reported no meaningful impact on writing from these kinds of reading experiences. Lacking the kind of structure or guidance provided in the direct model of reading for writing, many learners relying on free reading experiences may not be equipped to learn well about writing from reading. Of particular importance may be such variables as the age and language proficiency level of students when they engage in free, voluntary reading, as well as the kinds of texts they select for such reading. Another important factor is the kind of writing students are expected to do after their reading. For instance, pleasure reading of novels may not help students in their writing of, say, lab reports for a science class. Hence, teachers interested in encouraging students to engage in free, voluntary reading need to consider carefully what it is they want students to achieve and whether some guidance should be provided while still maintaining the free nature of the reading.

Conclusion

Here, as in Chapter 3, we examined the idea of approaching reading-writing connections from a directional perspective in which we favor or emphasize one of the skills in order to lead to better learning of the other one. The fundamental advantage of this directional perspective is that, from the critical point of view of developing pedagogical tasks and selecting teaching and learning materials, we have a clear-cut starting point—that is, we know whether we want to use writing to strengthen reading (Chapter 3) or reading to strengthen writing (this chapter). This knowledge will play a crucial role in deciding how we want to proceed with our students, and for many teachers, it may (understandably) be necessary to have this kind of established starting point to work from. But of the two approaches—writing for reading or reading for writing—which is the better choice? There is in fact no definitive answer to this question, as a number of variables come into play when trying to make such a decision. Much will depend, of course, on the already existing strengths and the needs of one's students.

With respect to our focus in this chapter, we do need to bear in mind some limitations to using reading for writing. For instance, in the case of the reading models approach, Smagorinsky (1992) points out that "the study of a product simply cannot *teach* a writing process" (p. 162); that is, directing students' attention to writing-based features of texts and how those features operate to create effective writing does not ensure that students will make the leap from effective reading to effective writing. As Devine (1993) observes, in the case of L2 writers, in particular, "they may not have the appropriate declarative, procedural, and conditional strategic knowledge needed to support completion of the task" (p. 120). In other words, even if students learn a good deal about L2 writing from their reading, they may still lack the ability to effectively apply that knowledge, especially because what they're being asked to do with the information acquired may be unfamiliar to or quite difficult for them. For instance, to return to Chapter 3 and the focus on summarizing and synthesizing, it may well be that what these tasks actually require for completion may be hard for students to grasp, especially those students who are newer to L2 writing.

This is why, says Hunt (1985), "we cannot simply use texts

to teach writing; we have to teach reading as well—that is, we have to find ways to help students learn how to read in order for them to be able to use reading as a tool for learning to write" (p. 162). This is partly because we cannot assume that "reading is the same process for all readers" or that "a textual device will have essentially the same impact and influence on any reader" (Hunt, 1985, p. 160). In reading-for-writing work, then, we must be careful not to focus too heavily on what we want students to learn about writing from their reading; we must also ensure that they're properly prepared for the kind of reading necessary to extract information about writing. In this view, we cannot simply assume that students are ready to learn about writing from reading.

In the case of both the direct and indirect models of reading for writing, then, we need to lay some groundwork for the work students will be doing. Here are some suggestions:

- Discuss with students, before reading begins, the kinds of support work they can do during their reading, such as taking notes on the rhetorical and linguistic characteristics of the material they're reading or using a highlighting pen to denote those features. To increase the effectiveness of this approach, we can demonstrate it in class using, for example, transparencies to mark off important writing-related material in sample tasks. These demonstrations can be accompanied by class discussion of the process. Students can then be asked, individually or in groups, to duplicate the process.
- Provide charts students can fill out (as or after they read) and then study before moving on to any writing tasks based on their reading. In these charts, they could record any rhetorical strategies they see in the texts they read and/or could give examples of specific linguistic devices used, such as words and

phrases used by authors when signaling arguments used in their essays.

- Before reading begins, carefully review the requirements of the writing task to be performed following the reading activity, such as what is expected in a summary. In this way, students are particularly well prepared to go on to their reading.

Some key points to bear in mind in employing a reading-for-writing approach are:

- If we want students to learn about writing from reading, special attention must be paid to the kinds of *input* we provide through reading. This point applies to both the direct and indirect models of reading for writing—though, by definition and nature, the direct model requires more explicit control over the selection of texts to be read.
- Our decision as to whether to work within a direct or indirect model depends heavily on whether we believe students gain more meaningful information through conscious learning or subconscious acquisition; that is, the learning/acquisition distinction plays a central role in learning about writing from reading, and as teachers we need to know where we stand with respect to this distinction and its application in the context of reading-writing connections.
- As noted earlier, we cannot assume that there is an automatic transfer of knowledge of writing gained from reading to the act of writing. Even if students learn a great deal about writing in the target language through their reading, application of that knowledge is a challenging task for many students. Thus, we need to pay attention in our classrooms to the movement from reading for writing to actual writing. Having students express, in writing, what they have

learned about writing from their reading is one important way of doing that, but this is probably not sufficient in many cases. Having students describe, verbally or in writing, the writing task they will eventually perform is a primary way of looking into applications of knowledge gained through reading. If, for instance, we are asking students to write an argumentative essay, we can first have students tell us, *in their own words,* what that task requires them to do. We can discuss what they have learned relative to that writing task during their reading.

Like writing for reading, reading for writing probably has some intuitive appeal to many teachers, especially since many of them may well have learned about writing (L1 or L2) through their reading. Both the direct and indirect models offer valuable opportunities for learning about writing for reading. While there is perhaps no definitive research that supports the belief that reading improves students' writing by exposure to target language writing, it appears reasonable to assume, as many specialists have pointed out, that good writers generally are good readers—that is, that they have learned about writing through reading, that reading has taught them about writing or has prepared them to write by empowering them with knowledge of writing. Thus, our main task in a reading-for-writing context is to decide (a) whether we believe the direct or indirect model will best serve the interests and needs of our students and (b) what support work we can do to try to ensure that students can meaningfully apply to their writing what they have learned through their reading.

Questions for Reflection and Discussion

1. On p. 111, I quote Leki's remark that "reading is what makes it possible for us to write, rather than the other way around." What's your response to this assertion? Why?

2. To which of the two major models of reading to write—the direct or indirect model—do you find yourself more attracted as learner and/or as teacher? Why?

3. To what extent does Krashen's observation (quoted on p. 112) that "it is reading that gives the writer the 'feel' for the look and texture of reader-based prose" match your own experiences of reading and writing in your L1 and/or L2; that is, how much has reading contributed to your own development as a writer?

4. What's your reaction to the notion of extensive reading? Do you believe it can help L2 students as much as its supporters claim? Is it better to focus on intensive reading schemes, where students concentrate on close reading of a few texts rather than the wider reading advocated in extensive reading schemes?

5. The thesis of this chapter is that *input* gained through reading is essential to L2 writing development. To what extent do you agree with this thesis? Why? If you disagree, what do you see as a more powerful source of writing development?

6. What's your response to Krashen's "pleasure principle" (p. 133) and his belief in the power of free voluntary reading? Why?

Chapter 5

Models of
Reading-Writing Pedagogy

In this chapter we'll look more closely at what it means to explore reading-writing connections in the classroom context. While Chapters 2–4 offered some teaching suggestions relative to their specific focuses on reading-writing relations, there is more to be said about reading-writing connections pedagogy, which is the purpose of this chapter. This will be done mainly by examining several models of reading-writing connections instruction. Key features of each model are described, followed by comments on the implementation of each model with respect to selecting instructional texts and tasks.

Whichever model a teacher adopts, it's important to remember that when reading and writing in academic settings, students are primarily engaged in *composing from sources,* a point that undergirds much of what is presented in this chapter; that is, their writing is usually based on some type of reading. Another vital preliminary point to bear in mind is that the models and types of pedagogical activities suggested in this chapter are amenable to both the traditional print-based and more contemporary electronic reading-writing environments. In other words, teachers can work within the three essential modes of *response, writing for reading,* or *reading for writing* (discussed in earlier chapters) regardless of whether the sources used are conventional print texts or online texts in a computer-mediated environment, though nuances specific to these environments may change how teachers and students operate within these modes.

Of course, what we do with respect to adopting a model to work with and selecting texts and tasks will depend to a large extent on the kinds of students we're working with, the school level or setting in which we see them, and what they need to accomplish in their L2 writing and reading. What we do with new learners of English in, say, the elementary school classroom will clearly not match how we teach students in a graduate-level academic writing course. On the other hand, there are certain core principles we can follow whatever the circumstances at hand. Acquainting readers with these principles has been one of the goals of the book. For instance, in our practice we should strive to:

- Teach reading and writing together, not separately.
- Show students that both reading and writing are acts of composing, of meaning making.
- Demonstrate how reading supports writing and writing supports reading

    (a) by using reading to create an acquisition-rich environment for writing development and
    (b) by using writing to provide a way in to reading and reading development.

- Allow students to perform reading-writing tasks that are meaningful to them.
- Create opportunities for students to talk about reading-writing connections.

Pedagogical Models

Computer-Mediated Model

To appreciate this approach to reading-writing connections pedagogy, we first need to place the model in context, as Donald Leu does in the following summary of how the landscape for academic reading and writing has changed in recent years:

Fifteen years ago, students did not need to know word processing technologies. Ten years ago, students did not need to know how to navigate through the rich information environments possible in multimedia, CD-ROM technologies. Five years ago, students did not need to know how to search for information on the Internet, set a bookmark, use a web browser, create an HTML document, participate in a mailing list, engage in a collaborative Internet project with another classroom, or communicate via e-mail. Today, however, each of these technologies and each of these environments is appearing within classrooms, forcing teachers, students, and researchers to continually adapt to new definitions of literacy. (Leu, 2000, p. 759)

In this environment where reading and writing interact, the notion of *electronic literacy*—that is, the demands and skills necessary to read and write texts in online circumstances where a computer screen, rather than a traditional print form of text, dominates—is crucial. As Warschauer (1999) explains, "Electronic literacy involves not only adapting our eyes to read from the screen instead of the page but also adapting our vision of the nature of literacy and the purposes of reading and writing" (p. 13).

Meanwhile, our students likely operate in the world of conventional *print literacy* as well, thus creating a situation in which writing teachers must increasingly account for both the print and electronic domains of reading and writing activity. As we make this "transition from traditional print literacy to multilayered, computer-based literacy" (Selfe, 1989, p. 8), we as writing instructors need to find a workable classroom balance between teaching the old and new ways of reading and writing—that is, how to read and write in the old and new environments of academic literacy. We need to locate what Tuman (1992) calls "the best of both worlds, the intensity of the page and the play of the screen" (p. 110), that is, classroom practices that help learners read and write conventionally ("intensity of the page") and electronically ("play of the screen").

As noted earlier in this chapter, the three reading-writing connections modes discussed in Chapters 2–4 apply to both print and electronic literacy. Students can just as easily respond, write for reading, or read for writing in both the print text and electronic text environments. There are, however, nuances of electronic literacy that must be examined if we are to fully understand reading-writing relationships and the teaching of them in the 21st century.

Slatin (1990), for example, speaks of the "multiple points of entry, multiple exit points, and multiple pathways between points of exit and exit points" (p. 870) when students read texts via the Internet, particularly in the increasingly popular hypertexts that students encounter when they conduct electronic searches for information. In these circumstances, students must navigate numerous links as they move from one website to another, as in a hypertext document. However, as they do so, they may encounter what Haas and Hayes (1986; see also Haas, 1989) have called the "getting the sense of the text" problem; that is, electronic texts, because they're screen-based, may require the use of reading strategies different from those that students are accustomed to employing while engaging print texts. Where does one start and stop when reading electronically, especially while jumping among a host of websites and links? Readers may not be able to find one particular text, with a clear-cut beginning, middle, and ending, from which to center their reading and gain the sense or guidance essential to *focused and productive reading activity.* Hence, L2 readers not already highly computer literate may be confused by the textual worlds they've entered and thus struggle to "get the sense of the text" as they wander, without the guidance provided by print texts, from link to link or website to website. It's not difficult to imagine the challenges faced by many L2 readers when they read via a computer screen and face a sea of computer links with no directions to follow while traversing them.

In addition to being a reading problem, this "getting the sense of the text" dilemma may present writing problems as well, in that students may not be equipped to write about these new kinds of texts in light of the challenges related to reading them. For instance, it may be more difficult to summarize or synthesize a series of computer links than a set of print texts laid out neatly next to or in front of the student as she writes. Writing problems may also occur in having to create electronic texts, such as homepages or hypertexts, with their embedded links to other texts. Here, too, students might lack the rhetorical guidance that may come more naturally with traditional print text types such as essays, where the beginning, middle, and end are clearly defined. Another way in which this is expressed in the professional literature is to say that print texts are *linear* in nature, while electronic texts are often *nonlinear*. Reading and writing in a linear way—proceeding systematically from beginning to middle to end—may be easier for many students than the nonlinear, or less structured, way common in the world of electronic texts.

Given these reading-writing conditions, a computer-mediated model of reading-writing connections pedagogy is one in which students operate in a screen or online culture rather than a print culture and so learn how to perform acts of composing requiring different, or nonlinear, ways of conceptualizing reading-writing connections. Instructional activities can include discussion of what is involved in reading and writing electronically and how the demands of this textual domain differ from those in the print text world as well as actual reading and writing of electronic texts. What is essential in this model is to look at what it means to compose—in reading as well as writing—via computer.

Teaching within a computer-mediated model does not exclude the activities traditionally associated with writing instruction and reading-writing connections work: summarizing, synthesizing, responding, and so forth. Furthermore, this model is equally appropriate in the three modes of reading-writing connections pedagogy explored here: response, writing for reading, and reading for writing. Students can perform in the computer-mediated environment any of the tasks we normally associate with reading and writing. What the computer-mediated model allows, through its emphasis on non-linear ways of reading and writing, is the opportunity to look at how to conduct the acts of reading linked to writing relative to the limits and opportunities associated with engaging texts onscreen rather than in print. For example, how does one synthesize a series of electronic texts after reading and processing them onscreen rather than by conventional hard copy?

Meanwhile, there are activities students can only perform in the computer-mediated environment, such as website or homepage construction, and teaching students what reading and writing mean while constructing these kinds of texts is also the business of the computer-mediated model. Here is where we use this model to highlight the new and different demands, challenges, and opportunities for students as writers/readers as they enter the world of electronic texts. For instance, as Shirk (1991) has noted, in the nonlinear world of electronic literacy, the reader/writer must be an "architect of information" (p. 200). As a reader, she or he must make sense of and manipulate a world teeming with possible pieces of information (located in various computer links and appearing in nonlinear fashion) to be used in writing; and as a writer, she or he must be able to (a) learn about writing in this nonlinear world through her or his reading activity (i.e., reading for writing) and (b) assemble the appropriate pieces of information in a meaningful way in her or his own written text. By seeing these kinds of activities conceptualized as being akin to the work of an architect (to return to Shirk's term), we are presented with a somewhat different notion of the "composing model of reading and writing" that has dominated this book, though the differences are not easy to quantify or articulate (nor are the notions mutually exclusive). One way to capture these differences might be to say that the "composer" of texts (working in the print text culture) is using the overlapping processes of reading and writing to directly *create meaning,* while the "architect" of texts (working in the electronic text world) is assembling and maneuvering blocks of information (i.e., different texts) that future readers and writers will then engage and make meaning from. The focus here is more on *generating meaning potential* through the various options represented by the links embedded in the electronic text produced. That potential is to be unraveled later, as readers/writers plan their own journey through the links in the text(s). This is in line with the more open-ended, nonlinear nature of online texts.

Another way of conceptualizing the computer-mediated model is to think of it as constituting a different *environment* in which reading-writing connections are enacted. The key characteristic of that environment has already been discussed briefly—its fundamentally screen-based, nonlinear nature. Here students move away from the conventional print-based, linear environment of traditional writing instruction. By adding a computer-mediated model to our repertoire of possible reading-writing pedagogies, we enlarge the notion of writing instruction itself because we bring into play this deeper notion of an environment in which reading and writing take place. An environment is a place with its own rules, conventions, practices, tendencies, and so forth. If we confine writing instruction to the print-based world, reading and writing are basically only actions to be performed relative to the expectations of that world. When we instead opt for an environmental conceptualization of writing instruction, one where there are both print-based and electronically based choices, as well as linear and nonlinear choices, we ask students to examine the atmosphere or context in which reading and writing take place, not just the activities themselves. At a time when more and more students are expected to read and write both conventionally and electronically, we face an obligation as writing teachers to expose our students to these different composing *environments,* not just to different reading and writing techniques. The computer-mediated model makes this possible.

To gain a better sense of the computer-mediated model, it is worth reviewing some of the primary features, as well as benefits, of this pedagogy for linking reading and writing:

- It can create an even closer link between reading and writing *as acts of composing* (in addition to its "architect of information" emphasis) because of the nature of online reading and writing. For instance, when students conduct computer searches for source text material to be included in an act of writing, such as an argumentative essay, they take on added authority as readers while performing web searches and deciding which links to pursue and which links to make (in both their reading and the text they write, which might include its own links to other texts). In this sense, they are more actively writing, or composing, their readings than is usually the case with reading in print culture. In this way, they can see how reading, like writing, is an active process of constructing meaning as opposed to the more passive decoding of already existing meaning, particularly as they reflect on the choices they've made in selecting and working with links.
- The computer-mediated model opens student literacy activity to a wider array of text types to read and write. While students in a computer-mediated environment have access to all of the text types available in print culture, they can access electronic texts as well by negotiating the links in hypertexts and hypermedia documents. In online culture, they may be "reading" links that are visual (e.g., videos) or aural (e.g, music) in addition to sources presented in print form (albeit on a screen). Likewise, they have an expanded repertoire of text types to choose from as writers. They can still compose conventional essays or construct complex hypertexts consisting of multiple links to other sources. Recording or discussing, in writing, what they have encountered in their "reading" can thus take on new dimensions or create new challenges and opportunities for written expression related to reading.
- Because the computer creates constant access to teachers and classmates (and electronically based

support materials such as online writing centers or services) via e-mail, chatrooms, listservs, and so on, and because this access can occur via multiple locations (computer labs, home computers, etc.), the computer-mediated model reshapes and expands the notion of the "writing classroom." The reading and writing that students perform for a writing course by employing the computer-mediated model can occur at any time, rather than within the more prescribed hours of a class session and in the more traditional confines of a classroom, and students can share their reading and writing under widely varying conditions. Essays, peer review comments, and dialogue with classmates and/or the instructor can occur at any time. As a result of this convenience of composing, students may feel more motivated by and interested in their reading and writing, particularly since they have more control over how and when it takes place.

- At a time when, increasingly (in many cultures), computer skills and computer-based literacy are required in the workplace, L2 writing classrooms featuring a computer-mediated model of reading and writing can better prepare students to read and write in occupational contexts.

- Because student decision making is increased in a computer-mediated reading-writing environment (e.g., in deciding which links to explore while reading in cyberspace), L2 writers may feel empowered as readers/writers in ways not as easily experienced in print culture.

- The screen-based nature of computer-mediated reading and writing, together with the advantages and disadvantages associated with composing within the domain of a screen, can create meaningful opportunities for discussion of the demands and challenges of reading and writing. Students can, for example, be asked to discuss the differences between print and online reading and writing and to debate the merits of the two cultures, leading to heightened awareness of reading and writing and their connections. As they compare and contrast online and print reading and writing, students can focus intensively on each environment or culture and enrich their understanding of the various dimensions of reading and writing.

Comments on Selecting Texts and Tasks in the Computer-Mediated Model

Selection of texts to be used and tasks to be performed in the computer-mediated model can be an especially challenging as well as interesting task for writing teachers. This is partly because there are so many text types to choose from. For instance, the source texts used need not be online texts, even though what is done with them is ultimately computer-mediated in the form of writing. In other words, students can be asked to work with conventional print texts. They can also be asked to work with a combination of print- and screen-based texts. This combination is especially attractive because it allows for meaningful discussion of linear and nonlinear reading and writing. Teachers can also opt to work strictly with online texts, in which case they, too (like their students), must be prepared to navigate the complex assortment of links available on whatever topic is being used, in order to design assignments effectively and help students engage them.

Such staples of reading-writing connections pedagogy as summarizing, synthesizing, and responding can be performed in a computer-mediated environment as easily as in a print-based environment, as noted earlier. Indeed, these activities might be easier to enact because of the added convenience the computer provides in terms of revising written work. Peer review of the reading of source texts (where students discuss the texts while reading them) and/or writing about them can be performed via computer in a computer lab or by e-mail or another electronic mode of discussion. Students can also use the computer to compose group-generated writing based on print texts. Some of the most exciting and rewarding moments in my career as a second language writing teacher have occurred while watching students clustered in small groups around a computer in a computer lab as they collaborate in summarizing, synthesizing, or responding to source texts. The ability to revise writing quickly and easily by computer while taking into account the views and suggestions of their classmates as they together peruse the source texts and previous drafts of their writing represents for L2 students a compelling blend of reading and writing not easy to duplicate in non-computer-mediated approaches to writing instruction.

Text and task selection in this model is also challenging as well as interesting because students' level of experience and comfort with online reading and writing may vary considerably. In this sense, working strictly within print culture for the selection of source texts is the easier approach (even when the writing occurs via computer), in that it is generally safe to assume that students are familiar with reading and writing in this culture (though this may change radically in the near future). Though it is becoming more common to find students whose primary medium of writing is the computer (and who thus may be inclined against pen or pencil writing), the use of print-based source texts for instructional purposes is generally still common enough to put all students on equal ground. On the other hand, some students are likely to feel more comfortable with online reading and writing than others. It may eventually be the case that all students will be highly computer literate and prefer online reading and writing, but in many school settings, that is not true at present. Thus, to require students in a writing course to read and write online only, or primarily, may create a classroom ecology that privileges some students over others and intimidates some while motivating others. Therefore, in deciding what kinds of texts students will read and what kinds of tasks they will perform (particularly in the case of tasks that are solely computer-mediated, such as webpage authoring), teachers inclined toward a computer-mediated model might need to do more in terms of learning about student attitudes and experiences toward reading and writing than was the case in the past, when all texts and tasks were print-based.

Text and task selection in the case of online texts will also be affected to some degree by the extent of students' computer literacy skills. If, for example, students are to be required to access web pages in search of source text material to be read and written about or to create their own web pages, attention must be paid to helping students negotiate such tasks. Those with few or no previous experiences of this kind will clearly need help not only in finding web pages but in coping with the links they will encounter, as well as in the technical details of website construction when engaged in their own writing. Furthermore, because of the range of texts a web page may link with and the varying quality of those texts, students need assistance in learning how to select texts or links for their own use, particularly since cultural boundaries or differences may prevent them from effectively analyzing what they find. For example, while working in an undergraduate ESL writing course with Elie Wiesel's book *Night,* about a boy's attempt to survive life in Nazi concentration camps, my colleagues and I found that some students were not only accessing but citing, as authoritative texts, material from groups claiming the Holocaust never occurred. For students not especially familiar with the Holocaust, it's difficult to know which links and texts are appropriate for academic reading and writing tasks. This type of situation can occur with many of the topics used in writing courses.

With regards to the use of online texts, then, task selection may need to include support activities that teach students *how* to read and write online. This applies not only to learning how to discriminate among the many types of texts available online but also to learning how to read and write—that is, to compose—within the nonlinear confines of screen culture. Given that online texts can only be read one screen at a time and that access to other pages (in the recursive movement back and forth through texts that is essential to quality reading) is more difficult to achieve in online than in print culture, tasks that help teach online reading may be essential. Because composing from sources (in various forms) is such a crucial part of academic writing instruction and because rules governing intellectual property rights where electronic texts are concerned are still under construction and may be unknown by students or difficult for them to apply (Bloch, 2001), task selection in the computer-mediated model can also include activities that discuss what constitutes plagiarism when composing from electronic texts. (See Barks and Watts, 2001, for a helpful illustration of such activities.)

In my earlier discussion of the features and benefits of the computer-mediated model, reference was made to the potential for student comparison and contrast of print and online reading and writing. Here, there is considerable room for selection of meaningful texts and tasks. Students can be assigned both print and electronic texts and asked to compare and contrast their reading strategies and difficulties when encountering such texts, just as they can be assigned tasks that require them to comment on print and computer-based writing. How they compose from both kinds of source texts and, in the process, link reading and writing can also be a subject of discussion. These can of course be oral discussions in class, but writing can also be used as a medium of reflection and exploration, including reflections shared electronically via listserv, webCT, or chatroom forums.

What seems clear, then, is that creating space for student *discussion* of online reading and writing may need to be a central principle of text and task selection in the computer-mediated model. To a certain extent, this is a need in any reading-writing connections work, since L2 students are encountering reading and writing situations and demands that are new or not very familiar to them. Opportunities to talk about what they're experiencing and about how to negotiate the new forms of reading and writing, whether print or electronic, are invaluable. However, online reading and writing, being screen-based and sometimes nonlinear in nature, present students with literacy challenges unlike those found in conventional print-based writing and reading. These challenges need to be addressed in selecting texts and tasks within the computer-mediated model.

Literature/Response-Based Model

As discussed and briefly demonstrated in Chapter 2, this model revolves around students writing in various response-based modes, such as reading logs or journals, response papers, or, in the case of a technologically based pedagogy, an electronic discussion format in which students post comments via a course listserv, webCT, chatroom, and so forth. Tasks revolve around written responses to assigned literary texts. Selection of texts would depend largely on the ages, language proficiency, and needs of learners. A significant advantage of this model is that it can be used in virtually any instructional setting. As seen in books by Franklin (1999), Hudelson (1989), and Peregoy and Boyle (2001), to name a few representative texts, literature can be a wonderful resource for children in the context of emergent literacy; that is, reading and writing about literature make possible meaningful literacy experiences early in their acquisition of L2 reading and writing skills, at a crucial period in their development, when strong associations and preferences for learning modes are being formed. Stories have a particularly powerful appeal for children through their unique ability to tap into children's imaginative capacities. There is something about narrative, about the structure of storytelling, that captivates both readers and writers and thus increases motivation to read and write. Therefore, by reading stories and responding to them, as opposed to experiencing a steady diet of grammar and pronunciation drills, children are more likely to associate pleasure and perhaps personal investment with the acquisition of L2 literacy skills, which may thus enhance the acquisition process. Reading and then composing their own poems can have the same effects. Making these early and formative encounters with L2 reading and writing exciting and enjoyable is crucial to the development of L2 literacy skills. By drawing from the endlessly rich field of children's literature, for example, teachers can then ask students to read and write poetry or short stories or can have them write journal entries sharing responses to them.

A literature and response-based model fits closely and comfortably with a major shift in elementary school pedagogy to the well-known whole language approach to teaching and learning. As Rigg (1991) explains of this approach, "The four language modes—speaking, writing, listening, and reading—are mutually supportive and are not artificially separated in whole language classes" (p. 526). The emphasis, she says, is on creating a comprehensive "language nurturing environment" (ibid.) in which students are immersed in the target language. In this kind of atmosphere, where the use of all four language skills in close conjunction with each other is the norm, it becomes natural to connect reading and writing activities. Talking about reading and writing also becomes important. As Huss (1995) points out, children acquiring reading and writing skills need opportunities to discuss their reading and writing so as to lend shape to their growing understanding of those skills. She advocates a "talk prior to writing" and "talk during writing" approach to instruction. Such talk makes writing and reading visible and generates opportunities for discussion of how the skills work together and of what children are learning about them.

As discussed in Chapter 4, extensive reading schemes are seen to promote L2 literacy acquisition, and these can be tied into the pedagogy just mentioned; that is, elementary school classrooms can have reading corners or other places where large numbers of literary (and non-literary) texts are available for students' voluntary reading and associated writing activities (e.g., their writing of short summaries of what they've read). Encouraging extensive reading (with connected writing activities) supports the whole language notion of saturating students with the target language and makes possible additional opportunities for children to talk about their reading and writing.

The principles and approaches just reviewed can be applied to new learners of English at the secondary school level as well. Because these students, like younger children, need to develop English language and literacy skills rapidly in order to succeed in their school subjects, it's essential for the

ESL instruction they receive to provide them with rich and meaningful exposure to the target language, including ways of reading and writing it. Custodio and Sutton (1998), noting that "students learn English when they are immersed in reading and writing" (p. 19), argue in support of a literature-based approach in which middle and secondary students read historical fiction and respond to it through written responses (as well as other forms of writing—e.g., poems and narratives of personal experiences), particularly in a content-based pedagogy where the literacy work is linked to what is being studied in history courses. Reading and writing about history through historically oriented literary texts can make history more interesting and meaningful for students while also exposing them to the target language. Performing this reading and writing in an ESL class setting also allows students to discuss, in an atmosphere that encourages such discussion, the form and meaning of the target language and the nature of literacy tasks required of them in other courses. Here again, the ESL course becomes a place where students can concentrate, in a supportive atmosphere, on the development of literacy skills required in other courses. In addition to reading and writing extensively, they can talk about that reading and writing. The richness of literary texts (in terms of language, content, and rhetorical schemata) can make that work more meaningful and thus motivate students because the stories at the heart of literature—with their plot twists, important moments or events, and interesting or appealing characters—lend themselves to written and/or oral discussion in ways other texts might not.

Much of the work with literature, especially in a response-based mode, has focused on college-level students who operate at upper-intermediate to advanced levels of L2 proficiency. Despite their higher level of proficiency, these students still need meaningful exposure to the target language as well as opportunities to see reading and writing as integrated skills, particularly since much of the work they do in content courses involves a combination of reading and writing. Ultimately, then, work with literature is aimed at enriching students' academic literacy skills, with written responses to literary texts seen as a valuable way of linking reading and writing. (For recent reviews on working with literature, see Belcher and Hirvela, 2000; Hirvela, 2001.) Approaches to literature and response-based reading and writing fall into three major categories: experiential, sequential, and collaborative.

The *experiential approach* is one in which the selection of texts for reading and tasks for writing center on students using the literary experience to reflect on their own lives and experiences. Vandrick (1997), for example, promotes the use of "diaspora literature," that is, literature that focuses on stories set in a wide range of locations (including students' home countries) rather than the culture of the target language and that explores themes with which students can relate personally. According to Vandrick, having students read and write about characters who face the same kinds of decisions the students themselves must make and having students integrate their own experiences into their written responses to the texts increase the chances for students to connect reading and writing. Because of their personal investment in the reading and writing, students are likely to pay closer attention to finding ways of making the reading and writing work together. Blanton (1994) and Costello (1990) have also presented cases for this combination of reading and writing involving students using their own experiences (at least in part) in framing their written responses to literary reading experiences. This approach could be equally valuable and effective among secondary school immigrant students, for whom increased understanding of conflicts and issues related to the transition to a new culture and language may be a pressing need. Whether students use their writing to respond primarily to the experiences of characters in texts or as a springboard to exploring their own experiences, these experientially based encounters with reading and writing through reading literature of personal relevance can create a natural bridge between the acts of reading and writing.

The *sequential approach* to literature and response-based reading and writing arises from a pedagogy explored most fully in the work of Spack (1985, 1994). Spack has students work through a sequence of writing tasks related to their reading that moves from pre-reading writing ("write-before-you-read") of a more unstructured nature to more conventional academic essays. Students first write about the themes of literary works before reading them, so as to enter the reading experience with some preparation for it. They move on to journal writing and response statements (like those advocated by Bleich and discussed in Chapter 2), to construct, through writing, early responses to reading. Succeeding assignments gradually become more formal or structured in orientation and approximate the kinds of writing modes common in academic writing (comparison-contrast, argument, etc.). Central to all these tasks is writing based on reading, so that the reading-writing connections are continually being made. Gajdusek (1988) has described a similar approach that, she says, has the key advantage of requiring "students to take responsibility for building their own successively more complex schemata (i.e., levels of understanding), which allow them to explore a text on successively more demanding levels" (p. 227).

A third major approach to linking reading and writing through a combined literature/response format is a *collaborative pedagogy* in which students work as communities of readers and writers negotiating literary texts (see, e.g., Hirvela, 1999b; Shulman, 1995). Here, the core reading and writing tasks are drawn from the other approaches just described. What differs is the emphasis on co-authoring of readings and writings. Shulman's approach revolves around peer review in which students compare both their pre- and post-reading writing about texts and then revise the composing of reading and writing while taking into account feedback received during the peer response sessions. Hirvela's approach also involves peer review, but under somewhat difficult experiences. In this approach, students work in groups over an extended period of time in their reading of and writing about a common literary text, with each group composing an essay. Thus, initial composing of readings and writings as well as revisions of the same are conducted as group exercises, with feedback from other groups playing a major role in the revision process. In this ongoing group and peer review talk about reading and writing, students are regularly required to reflect on their reading in connection with their writing in order to revise and strengthen the quality of their work.

Comments on Selection of Texts and Tasks for the Literature/Response Model

Texts in this model are obviously literary in nature, but the term *literary* is open to some interpretation. To some it means the traditional or canonical texts of a culture's established or prestigious literature. In the case of English, that would mean the work of such esteemed writers as Shakespeare, Dickens, Austen, Bronte, and so forth—that is, the writers of classic works. To others it means popular literature, such as mystery/crime novels, love stories, and so on—that is, "light" literature aimed at popular tastes and consumption and emphasizing entertainment, as opposed to the heavier or more substantial, meaning-driven content of canonical works. The distinction between genres—novels and short stories (fiction), poetry, drama—is also important to note. Except for poems aimed at children, where attractive rhythms and rhymes and themes are featured, poetry is generally believed to be a difficult genre for L2 students to cope with. Poetry of the kind considered suitable for students at the high school and college levels may feature complex organizational and linguistic structures that are difficult to process, in which case responses to texts are equally difficult to construct, as are the readings of the poems. Thus, particular care must be taken in the use of poetry for older learners, including not using poetry written for children, whereas for younger learners, the playful and entertaining nature of children's poetry can increase interest in reading and result in more motivated writing. Drama is an excellent genre in terms of content and generating written responses to the often compelling stories being told, but the reliance on dialogue, frequently quite colloquial in nature, can make dramatic texts difficult to understand and therefore difficult to write about. Fiction may be the most usable of the genres, in that well-chosen stories can feature appealing plots and attractive characters. Moreover, longer works of fiction require sustained reading and writing that can create more opportunities to link reading and writing.

Tasks used with literary texts within the response mode are, as noted earlier, likely to fall within such common and popular types as journals, reading logs, response statements in which students write initial or tentative responses to what they've read, and more formal essays in which students can develop a detailed response (including quotes from texts read) to themes, events, or characters in the texts. As was discussed previously, the writing can occur in a *pre-reading phase* (where students write about the subject matter or theme they know will be foregrounded in the text and thus activate schemata that they'll need for their reading of the text), a *during-reading phase* (where students write an ongoing series of responses to the text as they read, usually in the form of journal entries or reading logs), and an *after-reading phase* (in which students construct more elaborate and perhaps more formal written responses in the form of essays—e.g., response papers, argumentative essays in which they build support for a response, or synthesis papers in which they develop a discussion of a response by comparing and contrasting their responses to the text at different reading stages). To enhance the journal or reading log experience, having students exchange their writing and comment on it in written responses (in any or all of the three phases just mentioned) can be a good idea. I've long favored an approach in which students write on one side of a page and leave the other side blank so that classmates can compose responses to the entries during pair or group discussion sessions. When students respond to this more informal writing, they can reinforce reading-writing connections because their written responses are tied to classmates' readings of the text assigned. This draws attention to reading, and the use of writing to examine the reading creates a connection between the two skills.

Collaborative Model

As suggested earlier, in the references to Hirvela 1999b and Shulman 1995, joint reading-writing activity can work effectively in a group setting as well as an individual one. According to Bruffee (1983), "Traditionally . . . we assume writing and reading to be intrinsically individual, asocial activities" (p. 160). However, he says, "Although writing is enormously complex, it is basically a form of speech. To write is in effect to 'talk' to someone else in a focused and coherent way" (p. 165). There is, he says, an implied and ongoing dialogue taking place between reader and writer, one that causes the writer to construct writing as a form of speech. Given this fundamental link between speech and writing, it makes sense to create learning situations in which students talk about writing as well as practice writing. And, he says, to talk about writing "is not merely a helpful pedagogical technique incidental to writing. It is essential to writing" (ibid.).

Since, reading, like writing, is a form of composing, of meaning-making, it likewise makes sense to create classroom conditions in which students talk about their reading. Such talk helps them formulate more concrete understanding of their own readings of texts, and it exposes students to possible readings of texts that, serving as input, can reshape their own rereadings of texts and eventually direct their writing. In this process, then, as when they talk about their writing, students collaborate in the creation of meaning, and they model a form of composing.

Collaboration in the writing classroom often takes the form of writing group or peer review sessions in which students share and comment on drafts of each other's papers, with individual revision to follow (Carson & Nelson, 1994, 1996; Hedgcock & Lefkowitz, 1992; Liu, 1998; Liu & Hansen, 2002; Nelson & Carson, 1998; Nelson & Murphy, 1992, 1992–1993; Reid & Powers, 1993; Zhang, 1995; Zhu, 1995). This is a single author/group discussion format. In this form of collaboration, students end up talking not only about their work but about the principles and practices by which writing is conducted and measured. Because they're involved in an act of evaluation, they must compare drafts of essays to the standards and expectations representing quality writing of the type being composed. In addition, if such writing is based on reading, discussion of reading is also likely to take place in cases where the writing reflects an interpretation or use of a text that others find questionable or intriguing. Reading is reviewed in the process of reflecting on the interpretation or application in question. Finally, this type of collaboration lends itself to discussion of reading and writing together as students examine the quality of their inclusion of source text material in their writing. In these circumstances, says Reid (1993b), "Learners use each other's resources and work toward common goals; the result is the strengthening of the positive classroom climate and community" (p. 155). This approach to collaboration can be used with students at any level of education and language proficiency, with task selection and difficulty adjusted accordingly.

The other major approach to collaboration is captured in the title of a book by Ede and Lunsford, *Singular Texts/Plural Authors* (1990), where the emphasis is on group production of texts in which students collaborate as co-authors. From a reading-writing connections perspective, they can also collaborate both in their reading of source texts to be used in writing and in their discussion of how to move from reading of the source texts to writing with them. Sills (1988, pp. 24–25) describes three primary approaches to this type of collaboration from the perspective of writing:

1. The responsibility for drafting specific parts of a writing assignment, planned by the group as a whole, is delegated to individuals. The group then collaborates to revise and edit the parts into a single coherent whole.

2. Each member of the group writes a first draft of the whole assignment, which has been jointly planned by the group. All of the drafts are responded to and commented on by the group. A synthesis is arrived at

consensually by the group members, who then revise
and edit the final copy in concert.
3. A group of writers sits together and plans, drafts, and
revises a piece of writing, which thus becomes a single
response to the assignment.

A major advantage of this kind of approach, says Trimbur
(1989), is that "it organizes students not just to work together
on common projects but more important to engage in a
process of intellectual negotiation and collective decision-
making" (p. 602). Where reading-writing connections are concerned, particularly in the L2 context in which students are
still acquiring the target language, this process of negotiation
can play a pivotal role in linking reading and writing. As students discuss assigned readings (and in the process compose
new readings) and the writing that follows (or that occurs as
they read), they share their understandings of what it means
to read and write in the L2. Because composing in the L2 may
differ considerably from composing in the L1, opportunities
to talk through their perceptions and growing awareness of
reading and writing in the L2 are essential to second language
students. Relying on private, internalized conceptualizations
of L2 composing may limit what students can achieve in the
L2, since there is no active process of comparison and contrast with other conceptualizations. Engaging in this "process
of negotiation" requires students to reflect on what they know
in order to pass that understanding on to their co-authors in
meaningful and intelligent ways. Thus, what they already
know is put into a sharper perspective, and it may be extended or enriched by input acquired from the understandings shared by group members.

Furthermore, as Kenneth Bruffee (1984) has noted, "in the
long run collaborative learning models how knowledge is
generated, how it changes and grows" (p. 647). With respect
to reading and writing and their connections, what is mod-
eled as students collaborate in their discussions of what
they're reading and writing while co-authoring a paper is the
dynamic nature of the act of composing. In, say, a group of

four students co-authoring an essay based on reading, the group members will hear numerous accounts of composing as they discuss their interpretations of what they've read and their reactions to what they're writing, including how they're incorporating material from their source texts into their writing. This exposure to multiple acts of composing can serve as a valuable reminder of how active and subject to change acts of composing are and of how this dynamic nature of composing applies to reading as well as writing and to reading as connected to writing.

In this model of collaboration, then, "collaboration is more than teamwork," say Gergits and Schramer (1994, p. 187). The group production model makes possible what they call a "dialogic discourse" (ibid.) that enriches learning as negotiation and composing take place. An excellent pedagogical model of this is seen in Osburne and Mulling's (1998) textbook *Writing Together: A Project for Team Research*. Their approach, aimed at high-intermediate to advanced–level ESL/EFL students, requires students to conduct team research on second language acquisition involving the development of new vocabulary. Working in groups, students read three assigned articles contained in a companion anthology, gather their own data concerning vocabulary acquisition, and then collaborate in the writing and peer revision of papers incorporating the reading material and data from the team research. This kind of approach requires constant dialogue (or interaction and negotiation) among group members as they process their reading, design their study, analyze their results, and construct an academic essay that relates their data to what they've read. Reither and Vipond (1989) have discussed a similar "team research" approach to collaboration and see it as exemplifying the important and popular notion of "writing as social process" (p. 855).

Whichever of these collaborative approaches a teacher selects, they work from the same core belief captured by Schneider (1990): "Collaborative learning rests on assumptions of shared authority among group members and the notion that knowledge is socially constructed, not received. Even more fundamental is the assumption that through peer interaction, what individuals learn is more and qualitatively different than what they would learn on their own" (p. 36). As an opportunity for students to talk about L2 reading and writing and to share acts of composing, collaborative learning exposes students to deeper experiences of composing that can help instantiate in learners the principles and techniques of L2 composing. When reading and writing for and with their peers, as opposed to for their teacher, students may encounter more real or authentic composing experiences because the audience may seem more genuine (Belcher, 1990), and this may lead to more meaningful exposure to the ways in which reading and writing interact with and support each other.

As discussed in Hirvela 1999b in the context of literature-based group reading and writing, a key feature of the collaborative approach, however it is applied, is that it creates *communities of readers and writers.* Much of the reading and writing students perform is private in nature, which can make it difficult for students to examine or test the accuracy of their perceptions of L2 composing except in drafts of essays evaluated by teachers. The more natural give and take of composing is removed from the process. By contrast, creating a classroom that serves as a community of readers and writers engaging in the same reading and writing tasks makes possible the dialogue about literacy that learners need as their perceptions expand. A community-based pedagogy of group composing (in reading and writing) can "help students learn about reading and writing by allowing them to compare notes on what they believe to be effective reading and writing practices" (Hirvela, 1999b, p. 10). As part of a community of readers and writers and of learners, students can explore together and help each other unravel the mysteries and complexities of composing in the target language.

Like any pedagogy, collaborative reading and writing is not to everyone's taste, as Hoekje (1993–1994) and Kinsella (1996), among others, have pointed out. Working with others is often unwieldy, and students may be reluctant to express their ideas among classmates they don't know well or who come from cultural backgrounds different from their own, particularly if they feel insecure about their use of the target language. Then, too, there is the apparently common belief among L2 students that they learn from teachers, not each other. However much we, as teachers, may believe in the value of student collaboration, convincing students that this is a beneficial pedagogy is seldom an easy task.

Comments on Selecting Texts and Tasks in the Collaborative Model

As noted previously, the collaborative model lends itself to the use of any and all kinds of reading texts. L2 students can collaborate just as easily in the discussion of and writing about magazine or newspaper articles, scholarly articles, electronic texts, literary texts, and so on. On what basis, then, can texts be selected? The primary criterion for selection is probably the purpose for which students are writing, in that some text types may be more suitable for particular writing intentions. For instance, as seen earlier in this chapter, literary texts work especially well when response is the principal aim of writing, though nonliterary texts that focus on controversies can also lend themselves well to response-based writing. For example, high school or college students could be asked to read articles about a controversial and (to them) relevant topic such as proficiency or high-stakes testing, and they could write responses to arguments made for or against such testing. However, deeper or more sustained responses may well be generated in reaction to the themes, characters, and events in literary works, particularly since there is an interpretive aspect to such texts. Students collaborating in their reading of literary texts can trace, through writing, the development of their interpretations as well as their reactions as new events occur and as characters behave in response to those events.

On the other hand, if the ability to summarize or synthesize is the goal of writing instruction, nonliterary texts featuring a great deal of information will probably work best, since these texts will force students to perform close reading in order to identify which information should be summarized or synthesized. These kinds of texts are also useful in allowing students to discuss, in their collaboration, the rhetorical structures of source texts. Likewise, if their collaborative writing is intended to help them learn how to control or manipulate certain rhetorical structures common to traditional academic writing, these nonliterary texts will serve as better models for reading and writing work. Length of texts selected is also an issue. Assignments of shorter duration will clearly require shorter texts, whereas those intended to unfold over a longer period of time are well suited to longer texts, including books. Whatever the writing purpose for which texts are selected, a key issue in the collaborative model is whether the texts lend themselves to collaborative work. If students are going to collaborate, something in the text must leave open the possibility for different views or interpretations; otherwise there is little or no room for collaboration.

Task selection has already been hinted at in the previous comments. Students can work together composing summaries, syntheses, or responses. They could also prepare group outlines of texts read or, if the reading material is data driven, group analyses of the data. Earlier, we saw an example of a team research approach in which students write, collectively, the results of research they've conducted as well as a description of how the research was performed. Collaboration in the construction of a group essay or position paper is also useful, as is group construction of a website. All of these tasks could be employed with high school or college-level students and on a modified basis with younger learners.

Content-Based Model

References to this approach to instruction in Chapter 3 have already described its fundamental orientation: linking work in the L2 writing class to the writing-related tasks students perform in other courses. We saw in Chapter 1 that various surveys of academic writing tasks at the college level have provided some concrete sense of what students are expected to do in their (content) courses. As teachers, we also receive input from our own students about the writing-related expectations they face. It is possible, then, to develop course syllabi and instructional tasks based on this information. With its emphasis on connecting the writing course to what takes place in other courses, the content-based model, like the literature/response and collaborative models, is extremely well suited to attempts to link reading and writing. Where it differs is in its more overt concentration on the writing students must do in other academic contexts. Thus, a principal advantage of the content-based model is that it enables students to focus on the specific types of reading and writing—and the connections between them—that are relevant to their interests and needs as students.

There are three prevalent approaches to content-based writing instruction: theme-based, sheltered, and adjunct. All three are prominently described in the work of Brinton, Snow, and Wesche, particularly in their book *Content-Based Second Language Instruction* (2003). There they outline and exemplify, in great depth, the fundamentals of content-based instruction. They point out its roots in the fields of ESP and EAP, where instruction is based on the central idea of linking texts and tasks as closely as possible to the uses of language students will need to command in specific contexts of use. In ESP, for example, courses are designed to meet the linguistic and other language-related needs of students in such fields as nursing, law, accounting, and so forth. ESP is particularly well suited to creating courses addressing vocational language needs. EAP looks specifically at how language is used in academic contexts. (For more recent and comprehensive accounts of EAP, see Flowerdew & Peacock, 2001; Jordan, 1997).

As Brinton, Snow, and Wesche point out, the *theme-based approach* operates from a topic-oriented framework in which one particular topic (or theme) serves as the focus of the course. All texts and tasks are related to that topic or theme, and the topic or theme selected is ideally one that students will want or need to know about for other purposes. As an example, think about proficiency testing, a topic that will be of considerable relevance to many students, since such testing plays a significant role in many educational systems and school districts. Students in a content-based writing course organized thematically would be required to read a number of texts—and probably different text types—related to proficiency testing, in association with writing tasks incorporating material from those source texts. Because all of the reading and writing would revolve around the same common denominator or theme, the course would provide students with continuity, and continuity could, in turn, instill confidence as the students tackle the assorted reading and writing tasks. Rather than encountering a number of themes and, as a result, new vocabulary and concepts by moving among various topics (as is often the case in a writing course), students in this type of course will work with the same core vocabulary and content. This can lead to highly focused discussions of reading and writing and can help students better see the ways in which reading and writing activities overlap and connect. For instance, there could be detailed discussion of reading strategies to use in processing the different text types assigned (e.g., editorials, information-based articles, website-based newsletters, or essays from organizations supporting and opposing proficiency testing, such as parents' groups and teachers), just as there could be for the writing strategies or techniques necessary for different writing tasks assigned (journal or reading log entries responding to the readings, summaries, syntheses, student-generated editorials, etc.). Ways of directly linking the reading and writing could also be discussed. The consistency of theme throughout these discussions and, thus, students' increasing familiarity with the topic as the course proceeds would lend shape and meaning to the discussions and enhance the possibility of students making meaningful connections between reading and writing.

A second prevalent approach, the *sheltered course pedagogy,* likewise allows for more focused or sustained discussions of reading and writing. Here, L2 students are clustered in their own section of a content course, such as a psychology or history course. A more common example is probably that of college-level students enrolled in the usual required first-year writing course for undergraduates. In this case, L2 students would engage in the same course content and assignments, but within the shelter of their own sections of the course, taught by instructors interested in or more inclined toward working with L2 writers. The main advantage of such an approach is clear: students would be able to concentrate on those aspects of the assignments that their L1 counterparts might not need assistance with, such as grammatical or rhetorical features specific to certain kinds of writing tasks. Then, too, there could be the kind of discussion of specific reading and writing strategies noted earlier with respect to the theme-based approach. L1 students taking the course may not need instruction in how to read the assigned texts, whereas the L2 students would perhaps benefit from that more focused kind of instruction. While often discussed in the context of college-level courses, this approach to teaching and learning is especially helpful at the elementary and high school levels, where the L2 students might be much newer to the L2 than, say, ESL students at the college level. In addition to allowing L2 students more opportunities to acquire skills and knowledge already possessed by the L1 students, the sheltered approach enables L2 students to engage in such learning in what for many will be a more secure and comforting setting. From the reading-writing connections perspective, this approach once again makes possible increased opportunities for discussing interactions between reading and writing.

The third major approach, the *adjunct model,* has been particularly well described in the work of Johns, in addition to that of Brinton, Snow, and Wesche. In shorter papers (e.g., 1993, 1995) and her (1997) book-length treatment of a "socioliterate" approach to writing instruction, *Text, Role, and Context,* Johns has presented a persuasive case for the idea of directly linking a second language writing course to a specific content course; that is, L2 students taking the same content course (e.g., biology) could use the ESL course to discuss and complete the content course assignments. As Brinton, Snow, and Wesche (2003) explain, "every effort is made to dovetail the curricula of the language and content courses so that they maximally complement each other" (p. 60). This approach requires careful coordination between the L2 writing teacher and the content course instructor to ensure an effective connection between the courses. In what might be called a more orthodox application of the adjunct model, the teacher in the L2 course takes primary responsibility for identifying the linguistic and rhetorical focuses of the course, that is, the functions and tasks that the course will stress in an effort to prepare students to successfully negotiate the demands of the content course. If, for example, the content course requires students to read for and then write a term paper, the teacher in the L2 section of the course (perhaps in consultation with the content teacher or someone else in the field the course is situated in, the professional literature in EAP, or genre analysis) would direct students' attention to linguistic and rhetorical possibilities as well as to requirements specific to term papers. Reading and writing tasks would be geared toward providing meaningful practice in what students need to know to read and write well in the content course.

Johns's approach is a little different, in that it requires students, not teachers, to learn about what they need to know regarding writing and reading in the content course and the discipline in which it resides. Using the "student as ethnographer" concept and a genre-based framework, with a particular focus on the kinds of texts students must read and the tasks they must perform in the field the course represents, Johns asks students to research the content course's reading and writing practices and expectations and/or those of the discipline it represents and to report the results of their research. To return to the example of a term paper assignment, it would be the responsibility of students (with added input from the teacher, where necessary) to study the genre of the term paper so as to identify its key features and thus inform their own reading and writing related to that assignment. The L2 course then becomes a site for reporting and discussing what they have learned and for practice in performing reading and writing as practiced in the genre and the academic discipline being studied.

A key advantage of this approach to adjunct instruction comes from its genre orientation, in that what students learn about various genres of writing equips them not only to write (and read) for the content course the L2 course is aligned with but to work with the same genres in other course settings. As for reading-writing connections, this adjunct model encourages and empowers students to investigate what it means to read and write within a specific genre and discourse community. While researching the term paper, for instance, they can study models of term papers to look at how reading is applied within that specific genre as well as at the key writing-related characteristics of the genre, interview teachers to obtain relevant knowledge of reading and writing related to the genre in question, and in other ways gather valuable information about the genre.

Comments on Selecting Texts and Tasks in the Content-Based Model

The selection of texts and tasks in this model is clearly guided by what takes place in courses that the writing course is linked with. Indeed, the texts and tasks may to a large extent be decided on by content course teachers, although the writing teacher can be proactive in identifying roles and functions students can pursue. What may be especially important in this model, then, is the ways in which teachers gather information on which to base their teaching. As noted earlier, in the sheltered and adjunct approaches, cooperation with content area teachers is essential not only in the planning stages of a writing course. Working with content teachers throughout the duration of the course is important so that new input on assignments is always available. This can apply as well to the theme-based approach, in that writing teachers can consult with other teachers about the themes or topics dealt with in content courses. By knowing, for example, that students will eventually write about a specific topic—say, space exploration—the writing teacher can select texts and tasks that provide L2 students with a firm grounding in the topic and tasks often associated with it and, thus, can leave them better prepared to read and write about it later in another course.

The content-based model allows for use of other models of reading-writing connections work. This is an area where L2 writing teachers may have more latitude than in the case of selecting texts and core tasks; that is, writing teachers can pay particular attention to the *environment* in which content-based activities take place and can select a pedagogical model best suited to that environment. In order to maximize students' opportunities for learning about interactions between reading and writing, teachers can be on the alert for ways in which students best learn about these interactions. For instance, in some cases, the "singular texts/plural authors" collaborative concept may offer the best means of students experiencing reading and writing relative to a specific content course task or requirement. While the content-based model, because of its affiliation with other courses and perhaps other teachers, may offer writing teachers limited flexibility in terms of selecting texts and tasks, it leaves ample room for creating the best conditions in which to bring reading and writing together meaningfully for students.

Sequential Model

Another helpful approach to bringing reading and writing together is one that conceptualizes a writing course as a place where students work systematically through a carefully coordinated sequence of activities. At the heart of this sequential approach is the long-established idea of *scaffolding,* that is, the gradual construction of skills as students move through a series of tasks intended to steadily build knowledge and ability. One might say that each task is like a brick added to a foundation. As each task is completed, the foundation is strengthened or enriched, with succeeding tasks building on or extending the work achieved in the tasks preceding them. The sequences feature an important characteristic of reading-writing connections work already discussed: recursive movement back and forth between reading and writing through revisions of readings and pieces of writing. After students read a text or texts and write about them, they return to their reading as part of the process of writing a new draft of an essay, since the essay is linked to a source text or texts. There is, then, movement from reading to writing back to reading, and so on, with reading influencing writing and writing influencing reading.

The best-known application of the sequential approach, as mentioned in Chapter 3, is described in Bartholomae and Petrosky's book *Ways of Reading* (1987), which describes an undergraduate writing course developed at the University of Pittsburgh in the 1980s. The course grew out of their recognition that a writing course needs to account seriously for reading, since, as noted previously, academic writing normally involves writing based on reading, that is, the use of source texts.

Rather than have their students rush quickly from one writing assignment to another, with little or no discussion of reading (as happens so often in writing courses), Bartholomae and Petrosky organized their course around a series of topics or themes, with a controlled sequence of reading and writing tasks assigned for each sequence. These steps begin with informal responses to texts and gradually move through increasingly formal writing tasks, culminating in full-blown academic essays. In each sequence, students read several assigned texts and perform a variety of writing tasks—small and large, informal and formal—that involve a revisiting of the source texts while writing is being revised. Revision plays a vital role in each sequence. Students are required to complete a major essay in each sequence, supported by their earlier writing about their reading and by revision of the essay. In addition, at later points in the course, they are asked to compose reflection essays in which they revisit their earlier reading and writing in the course and comment on how it has contributed to their later work—that is, an exploration of the scaffolding at work in the course. There is, then, a carefully designed movement from one course sequence to another, so that scaffolding occurs not just through the activities performed during a sequence but also as students progress from an earlier to a later sequence.

Bartholomae and Petrosky's model was constructed within the L1 context; Leki (1991) and Spack (1993) have presented appealing applications within the L2 framework. Spack's (1993) model offers a frequently cited blueprint for a sequentially based L2 writing course for undergraduate students. Hers also involves scaffolding and recursive reading-writing movement, but from a somewhat different perspective. Citing the work of Carter (1990), Spack addresses what she sees as the need for L2 students to acquire both *general* knowledge of L2 writing—knowledge that can be applied in a variety of courses or academic settings—and *local* knowledge, that is, knowledge of writing within specific discourse communities. Thus, a writing course is seen as being organized along a continuum of activities intended to provide students with different skills and knowledge: "The continuum is developmental: The journey from novice to expert involves the acquisition of increasingly sophisticated frameworks of knowledge about composing" (Spack, 1983, p. 183). At the "novice" level, students acquire general knowledge about L2 composing; at the "expert" level, they learn how to write to meet the expectations of specific discourse communities. On a general level, her sequential approach works from this perspective:

> Composition instruction, then, must first aid students in the acquisition of general knowledge about writing and then move them back and forth along the continuum to grow as writers as they build enough local knowledge to enable them to perform effectively. Students' writing ability will continue to mature as they are influenced by numerous classroom experiences within and outside their declared majors. Mastery of the conventions of a specific discipline will come only through immersion in that field. (pp. 183–184)

The course itself is built on what she calls a "sequential, recursive syllabus based on reading and writing" that places considerable stress on "before reading" activity. The first step involves students using freewriting to explore a topic that will later be discussed in the source text(s) they will be assigned.

Spack believes that "this activity can stimulate interest in the reading. It also enables students to bring substantial background knowledge to the reading they are about to encounter" (p. 184). As the students go on to read the source text(s), they write, in the margins of the text(s), short annotations of the reading material, that is, phrases or sentences that record information about reading strategies employed or brief reactions to the text(s). They also write informal journal entries in which they respond in greater depth (than in the annotations) to what they're reading. The next step in the sequence is the writing of formal summaries of the source text(s), followed by in-class discussion of these summaries as well as the journal writing and annotations. With the scaffolding provided by these pre-, during-, and post-reading activities, students are ready to go on to the writing of a full-length essay on the assigned topic. This will include peer review activities and revision of the initial draft. Depending on the length of the course, students could potentially complete several sequences like this or focus on a few in greater detail, including discussion of discipline-specific writing features that would supplement the more general writing skills and knowledge acquired through the steps of the sequence just described.

Comments on Text and Task Selection in the Sequential Model

Scaffolding is central to both text and task selection in this model. Since sequences should produce a gradual buildup of skills and knowledge as students work through them and from one sequence to another, teachers need to bear in mind the complexity and impact of texts and tasks and where they fall within a sequence. It's interesting to note, for example, that Spack's approach begins with informal freewriting that allows students to write as they please and leads to more formal, structured writing such as summaries and, eventually, essays. And, as we saw earlier, she believes in the importance of (informally) activating learners' schemata about an assigned topic before actually confronting them with it in the assigned source texts. These are wonderful examples of scaffolding at work, and it is precisely this kind of movement from simple to complex, or informal to formal, that makes the sequential model so appealing, particularly from a reading-writing connections point of view. In other words, connecting reading and writing may be an easier task for teachers if they can move students through the kinds of sequencing already described, especially when complemented or supported by the classroom discussion of reading and writing noted earlier.

Selection of texts will be governed mainly by the ultimate aim of the writing sequence or the writing course itself. If the sequence or course is intended to build more general literacy skills and knowledge (to use Carter's [1990] dichotomy cited earlier), assigning a wider assortment of texts in terms of length, genre, and complexity may be advisable. This is what takes place in Bartholomae and Petrosky's pedagogy, where, in one sequence, students might be asked to read several texts of varying genres. Reading an array of text types will, for L2 writers, provide richer exposure not only to the target language itself but to its rhetorical variety. Because, as they move through other courses during their study (at whatever educational level), students will be exposed to various text types (depending on the nature of the courses), the more text types they read and write about in the L2 writing course, the better prepared they'll be for what occurs in these other courses. On the other hand, if the sequence or course is designed to emphasize local skills and knowledge, such as reading and writing in the context of history, text selection can follow more of a content-based approach and stress the selection of text types most commonly used in that genre.

Selection of tasks is influenced by the same factors shaping choice of texts, that is, the question of how wide or narrow the aims of the sequence or course might be. Hutchinson and Waters (1987) use the distinction between "narrow" and "wide-angle" ESP/EAP instruction, and Widdowson (1983) advocates selecting tasks along a "scale of specificity" ranging from a more general English orientation at one end of the scale or continuum to a specific purposes orientation at the other end. What we ask students to do, as well as what materials we ask them to use, will thus depend on the width of the sequence and course and on the amount of scaffolding we wish to see take place. In Spack's approach, "wide-angle" perspectives apply early in the sequencing, so we then see the informal and less structured writing mentioned earlier (freewriting, annotations, reading logs/journals). These kinds of tasks are not specific to any discipline or subject, so using them to analyze reading and to connect reading and writing will build general literacy skills and knowledge. The tasks later in the sequence—summary writing, perhaps syntheses, formal essays—are more focused in nature and can be linked to specific disciplines.

What we must watch regularly in the sequential model is the ways in which texts relate to other texts and tasks relate to later tasks (as well as how texts and tasks interact), so that we have the kinds of progressions from one text to another and one task to another that make a sequence effective. To be successful, a sequence must start in one place and lead students to another that follows naturally from the previous place. We have to know not only where we need our students to start and finish but which texts and tasks will enable them to move at an appropriate pace and to acquire appropriate skills and knowledge as they work through the sequence.

Building Reading-Writing Connections in Major Instructional Modes

Chapters 2–4 explored three baseline modes of academic reading-writing activity. Chapter 2 presented one mode rooted in the idea of *response;* Chapter 3 stressed a directional orientation using *writing to support reading;* and Chapter 4 emphasized activity moving in the opposite direction, *reading supporting writing.* We now look briefly at applications of the models of reading-writing pedagogy with respect to these three modes of activity.

The Response Mode

Here students link reading and writing through written responses to what they've read (thereby encouraging close reading of the source texts and drawing a tighter connection between reading and writing because this close reading fuels the written responses students compose), so our core task as teachers is to select texts and tasks that encourage response. The *computer-mediated model* is nicely suited to this mode in two ways. First, computer technology, particularly the networking function, provides an excellent medium through which students can share with classmates their responses to source texts. This might be via a course listserv, chatroom, newsgroup, or webCT discussion format. These networking functions provide a genuine and varied audience of classmates, thus adding incentive to writing because of the opportunity for communication with peers—authentic communication that students will have time to construct carefully because their thoughts are being shared in written, rather than oral, form and can thus be edited.

Second, the computer-mediated model makes possible an increased amount of writing based on reading—and thus links the two skills, because students can view a variety of comments from classmates. This is because successful course listservs and discussion groups will feature large quantities of student commentary, thus exposing students as readers/writers to a sizable and ongoing supply of texts to read and then respond to. And because they can do this at any time of the day, they may be encouraged to do more writing based on reading than would be the case in a print-based environment. Furthermore, by reading them carefully in the process of deciding which student messages or postings to respond to and which points within the selected messages to comment on, students function with care as readers and thus as writers and gain effective practice in writing based on close reading.

Closely aligned with the computer-mediated model in this mode is the *collaborative model,* in that students can interact with others while crafting responses to source texts they've read. For instance, students working in groups while writing essays can maintain easy and instant contact with each other, which should assist them in the writing process. In addition, they can provide, via a computer network, group (as well as individual) feedback on essays written by other groups and posted to the course network. They can also collaborate on group responses to assigned readings.

Finally, the *literature-based model* is ideally suited to response-oriented reading and writing because of the nature of literary texts. Stories are written to evoke responses. The characters and events found within them, as well as the themes they convey, should encourage students to write in response to what they've read.

The Writing-for-Reading Mode

We know from Chapter 3 that the essential feature here is the use of writing to assist reading (which, in the process, draws a connection between the two skills). All of the models discussed earlier would be useful. Through the *computer-mediated model,* students could (as in the response mode) use computer-based networking to share their writing about assigned texts and so build better understanding of the texts through the experience of reading each other's thoughts about or interpretations of the source texts. There is once again a natural link to the *collaborative model,* in that the networking framework creates, by its nature, a community of readers and writers negotiating (through writing) their reading of texts as they post their comments to a listserv, discussion board, and so on. As students encounter new ideas about or readings of the source texts through the posted comments on the network and then compose written messages conveying their own revised readings of the texts, writing is serving reading. As for the *literature-based model,* its contribution to the writing-for-reading mode is mainly in the kinds of content it can provide readers/writers. For L2 students, literary works in the target language may well prove difficult to understand, creating a strong need for writing (about the reading) intended to clarify the meaning of the source texts. The *sequential model* could lend itself to this mode by allowing students to construct written texts about assigned readings in a systematic way approximating a scaffolding approach. They could, for example, be given a series of readings of increasing levels of difficulty, perhaps on the same topic, and thus use writing to negotiate these challenges. They could also be asked to write increasingly sophisticated texts on an assigned topic (e.g., starting with annotations and ending in long essays). With respect to the *content-based model,* writing could be used to decipher or comment on source texts from the adjunct or content-subject field in question. If the assigned subject is one not very familiar to students, the source texts could prove to be challenging material, thus creating an added need for the use of writing to discover or unravel the meaning of the texts.

The Reading-for-Writing Mode

Here we use reading to learn more about writing in the target language. The *computer-mediated model* could be of considerable benefit because the computer's links to the Internet vastly increase the range of text types students can access. This greater access means that they have more source texts from which to learn about the characteristics of writing in the target language. There's also the matter of convenience. Instead of conducting labor-intensive searches for print texts, students can, via the computer, gain instant access (without having to leave their seat) to vast arrays of texts. The computer also has features through which students can easily and meaningfully highlight and in other ways analyze source texts. In this way, they can build their knowledge of how target language texts operate rhetorically and linguistically. And through computer networking, they can share what they learn about target language texts. Meanwhile, the *collaborative model* can come into play in this mode by allowing students to share the experience or process of learning about writing through reading. The *content-based model* can be helpful because it provides students with a focus on source texts in a specific (and hopefully relevant) field of study. In a writing course operating along ESP lines, this kind of emphasis would be particularly beneficial.

Conclusion

As a reminder of what we, as teachers, have to gain from the theories, research, and practices discussed in this book, let's close by briefly reexamining reading-writing connections from a few closely related perspectives. First, there is a more general statement from Ferris and Hedgcock (1998), who observe that "just as reading facilitates the development of writing skills, so writing can help build proficiency in reading" (p. 43). Here we see at work one of the principles undergirding comments made in all of the present book's chapters: that we can build a reading-writing connections pedagogy for students at any age and proficiency level by basing our practice (in part) on the idea that reading supports writing and writing supports reading. And through this supportive relationship, the two skills interact in ways that ultimately draw them together as acts of composing. This may be the most fundamental way of connecting the two skills in classroom settings. Text and task selection, as well as the choice of a model within which to center or locate them, can be built around the search for ways of helping students (a) use reading activities (e.g., use textual analysis to identify key rhetorical features of texts) to build knowledge that can be used in writing and (b) find writing activities (e.g., responding, annotating, summarizing, and synthesizing) that help students make sense of reading.

Next, we can take into account the following assertion by Scholes (1985): "Reading and writing are complementary acts that remain unfinished until completed by their reciprocals" (p. 20). In academic settings, whether at the elementary, high school, or college level, if we think of reading or writing activities as separate from each other and assign them with no thought toward linking them at some point, we prevent our students from seeing and experiencing these skills as true composing skills. Reading is perceived as simply decoding already existing ideas or information placed in texts by authors instead of as meaning-making that utilizes the constructive process writers employ when creating texts. Writing is merely the "correct" arrangement of words and ideas as dictated by certain rhetorical formulas rather than a creative process of establishing links to supplies of input, such as source texts, and negotiating new or extended meanings for that input in relationship to other ideas or input in the text being written. In other words, in academic contexts, we truly finish a reading when we write about it, in some way, either to revisit and rearrange our original reading or interpretation through writing about it, or by placing that reading in the context of other readings of other texts. We compose a reading when we think of it as we do an act of writing, and we compose writing when we incorporate into the written act knowledge gained from reading, whether knowledge of texts themselves or knowledge contained in them. Thus, in our teaching practice, we should look for ways of attaching a writing component (e.g., a summary or a reading log entry) to a reading assignment and a reading component to a writing assignment (by providing appropriate source texts that will influence the writing).

Another perspective that we saw from time to time in this chapter and in this book is reflected in Blanton's (1999) assertion that "in reading-writing classrooms, creating opportunities to interact with texts means engaging in tasks that require talking and writing about them" (p. 131). Here, "to interact with texts" can mean not merely reading them or writing them but writing about reading them or anticipating and thinking about writing while reading them. Instead of treating texts in isolation, we ask students, as much as possible and in ways discussed throughout this book, to combine reading and writing activities so as to experience the ways in which they connect. Meanwhile, "talking about them" is critical in the L2 context. L2 students need opportunities to break free from the private, individual ways in which composing so often takes place (i.e., alone in their room or the library), so as to put their own practices into more meaningful perspective by comparing and contrasting with the practices of their peers. This might occur through traditional peer review involving face-to-face discussion of their writing or through electronic review in which they share comments via an e-discussion format like a listserv or some other networking arrangement. Or it can mean simply talking as a class about how to read and write in the L2. The important point is to allow room for talk about composing.

Finally, recall Bartholomae and Petrosky's (1987) belief that "there is no better place to work on reading than in a writing course" (p. iii), a point that is at the heart of this chapter and this book. Recall also the comment from Carson and Leki (1993a) that "reading can be, and in academic settings nearly always is, the basis for writing" (p. 1). A second language writing course that fails to account for reading, as well as for its links to writing, impoverishes L2 writers. It doesn't direct their attention to the most important source of knowledge and input about writing—reading—and it doesn't help them learn about perhaps the most important tool in writing: the source texts that so much academic writing responds to or builds on. Unless we enable students to see how reading supports writing and writing supports reading (whether in print, online, or combined print/online environments), we leave them with an incomplete notion of writing. When, instead, we include reading in the writing course and discuss it as an equal partner with writing, we enrich our students' understanding of second language literacy and produce true *composers* and *architects,* that is, students who actively construct readings using the principles of writing and who thus learn about reading through writing and writing through reading. That should be our ultimate aim as L2 writing teachers.

Questions for Reflection and Discussion

1. Some L2 writing specialists object to the use of literary texts for academic reading-writing purposes, on the grounds that they aren't practical enough for the acquisition of academic literacy skills. What's your feeling about this? Why?

2. What are your own thoughts and principles of selection with respect to choosing texts and tasks for writing-reading activities?

3. Of the various models of reading-writing connections pedagogy reviewed in this chapter, which approach appeals most to you as a learner and as a teacher? Why?

4. What is your response to Bartholomae and Petrosky's assertion that "there is no better place to work on reading than in a writing course" (p. 37), particularly after reading the various chapters of this book?

5. As you conclude this book, how would you describe your own current or emerging philosophy toward reading-writing connections? What ideas discussed in this book have impacted most on the development of your present reading-writing connections philosophy?

6. What, in your view and experience, are the most important questions left unanswered or not yet satisfactorily answered with regard to L2 reading-writing connections?

7. What do you see as the strengths and weaknesses, as well as the opportunities and difficulties, of a computer-mediated approach to linking L2 reading and writing?

References

Ackerman, J. M. (1993). The promise of writing to learn. *Written Communication, 10,* 334–370.

Angelova, M., & Riazantseva, A. (1999). "If you don't tell me, how can I know?": A case study of four international students learning to write the U.S. way. *Written Communication, 16,* 491–525.

Applebee, A. (1992). The background for reform. In J. A. Langer (Ed.), *Literature instruction: A focus on student response* (pp. 1–18). Urbana, IL: NCTE.

Arndt, V. (1987). Six writers in search of texts: A protocol-based study of L1 and L2 writing. *ELT Journal, 41,* 257–267.

Barks, D., & Watts, P. (2001). Textual borrowing strategies for graduate-level ESL writers. In D. Belcher & A. Hirvela (Eds.), *Linking literacies: Perspectives on L2 reading-writing connections* (pp. 246–267). Ann Arbor: University of Michigan Press.

Barthes, R. (1989). *The rustle of language* (Richard Howard, Trans.). Berkeley: University of California Press.

Bartholomae, D. (1986). Wanderings, miswritings, misunderstandings. In T. Newkirk (Ed.), *Only connect: Uniting reading and writing* (pp. 89–118). Upper Montclair, NJ: Boynton/Cook.

Bartholomae, D., & Petrosky, A. R. (1986). *Facts, artifacts and counterfacts: Theory and method for a reading and writing course.* Portsmouth, NH: Boynton/Cook Heinemann.

Bartholomae, D., & Petrosky, A. R. (1987). *Ways of reading: An anthology for readers.* New York: Bedford Books/St. Martin's Press.

Bartholomae, D., & Petrosky, A. R. (1996). *Resources for teaching "Ways of Reading."* Boston: Bedford Books/St. Martin's Press.

Bazerman, C. (1980). A relationship between reading and writing: The conversation model. *College English, 41,* 656–661.

Bazerman, C. (1985). *The informed writer: Using sources in the disciplines.* Boston: Houghton Mifflin.

Beach, R. (1993). *A teacher's introduction to reader-response theory.* Urbana, IL: NCTE.

Beach, R., & Marshall, J. (1991). *Teaching literature in the secondary school.* San Diego: Harcourt Brace Jovanovich.

Belcher, D. (1990). Peer vs. teacher response in advanced composition classes. *Issues in Writing, 2,* 128–150.

Belcher, D. (1994). The apprenticeship approach to advanced academic literacy: Graduate students and their mentors. *English for Specific Purposes, 13,* 23–34.

Belcher, D., & Connor, U. (Eds.). (2001). *Reflections on multiliterate lives.* Clevedon, Avon: Multilingual Matters.

Belcher, D., & Hirvela, A. (2000). Literature and L2 composition: Revisiting the debate. *Journal of Second Language Writing, 9,* 21–40.

Belcher, D., & Hirvela, A. (Eds.). (2001). *Linking literacies: Perspectives on L2 reading-writing connections.* Ann Arbor: University of Michigan Press.

Belsey, C. (1980). *Critical practice.* London: Methuen.

Benesch, S. (2001). *Critical English for academic purposes.* Mahwah, NJ: Lawrence Erlbaum.

Bereiter, C., & Scardamalia, M. (1984). Learning about writing from reading. *Written Communication, 1,* 163–188.

Berthoff, A. E. (1983). How we construe is how we construct. In P. L. Stock (Ed.), *Fforum: Essays on theory and practice in the teaching of writing* (pp. 166–170). Portsmouth, NH: Boynton/Cook.

Blanton, L. L. (1993). Reading as performance: Reframing the function of reading. In J. G. Carson & I. Leki (Eds.), *Reading in the composition classroom: Second language perspectives* (pp. 234–242). Boston: Heinle & Heinle.

Blanton, L. L. (1994). Discourse, artifacts, and the Ozarks: Understanding academic literacy. *Journal of Second Language Writing, 3,* 1–16.

Blanton, L. L. (1999). Classroom instruction and language minority students: On teaching to "smarter" readers and writers. In L. Harklau, K. M. Losey, & M. Segal (Eds.), *Generation 1.5 meets college composition* (pp. 119–142). Mahwah, NJ: Lawrence Erlbaum.

Bleich, D. (1978). *Subjective criticism.* Baltimore: Johns Hopkins University Press.

Bleich, D. (1980). The identity of pedagogy and research in the study of response to literature. *College English, 42,* 350–366.

Bloch, J. (2001). Plagiarism and the ESL student: From printed to electronic texts. In D. Belcher & A. Hirvela (Eds.), *Linking literacies: Perspectives on L2 reading-writing connections* (pp. 209–228). Ann Arbor: University of Michigan Press.

Bloch, J., & Chi, L. (1995). A comparison of the use of citations in Chinese and English academic discourse. In D. Belcher & G. Braine (Eds.), *Academic writing in a second language: Essays on research and pedagogy* (pp. 231–274). Norwood, NJ: Ablex.

Bosher, S. (1998). The composition processes of three Southeast Asian writers at the post-secondary level: An exploratory study. *Journal of Second Language Writing, 7,* 205–241.

Boughey, C. (1997). Learning to write by writing to learn: A group-work approach. *ELT Journal, 51,* 126–134.

Braine, G. (1995). Writing in the natural sciences and engineering. In D. Belcher & G. Braine (Eds.), *Academic writing in a second language: Essays on research and pedagogy* (pp. 113–134). Norwood, NJ: Ablex.

Bridgeman, C., & Carlson, S. (1984). Survey of academic writing tasks. *Written Communication, 1,* 247–280.

Brinton, D. M., Snow, M. A., & Wesche, M. B. (2003). *Content-based second language instruction.* Michigan Classics Edition. Ann Arbor: University of Michigan Press.

Brozo, W. G. (1988). Applying a reader response heuristic to expository text. *Journal of Reading, 32,* 140–145.

Bruffee, K. A. (1983). Writing and reading as collaborative or social acts. In J. N. Hays, P. A. Roth, J. R. Ramsey, & R. D. Foulke (Eds.), *The writer's mind: Writing as a mode of thinking* (pp. 159–169). Urbana, IL: NCTE.

Bruffee, K.A. (1984). Collaborative writing and the "conversation of mankind." *College English, 46,* 635–652.

Burnham, C. C., & French, M. G. (1999). Writing to learn in science journals: Help for the "homeless in the universe." In S. Gardner & T. Fulwiler (Eds.), *The journal book for teachers of at-risk college writers* (pp. 73–89). Portsmouth, NH: Boynton/Cook Heinemann.

Campbell, C. (1990). Writing in others' words: Using background reading text in academic compositions. In B. Kroll (Ed.), *Second language writing: Research insights for the classroom* (pp. 211–230). New York: Cambridge University Press.

Carrell, P. L. (1983). Three components of background knowledge in reading comprehension. *Language Learning, 33,* 183–207.

Carrell, P. L. (1984). The effects of rhetorical organization on ESL readers. *TESOL Quarterly, 18,* 441–469.

Carrell, P. L. (1985). Facilitating ESL reading by teaching text structure. *TESOL Quarterly, 19,* 727–752.

Carrell, P. L. (1989). Metacognitive awareness and second language reading. *Modern Language Journal, 73,* 121–134.

Carrell, P. L. (1992). Awareness of text structure: Effects on recall. *Language Learning, 42,* 1–20.

Carrell, P. L., & Connor, U. (1991). Reading and writing descriptive and persuasive texts. *Modern Language Journal, 75,* 314–324.

Carrell, P. L., & Eisterhold, J. C. (1983). Schema theory and ESL reading pedagogy. *TESOL Quarterly, 17,* 553–573.

Carrell, P. L., Pharis, B. G., & Liberto, J. C. (1989). Metacognitive strategy training for ESL reading. *TESOL Quarterly, 23,* 647–678.

Carson, J. G. (1992). Becoming biliterate: First language influences. *Journal of Second Language Writing, 1,* 37–60.

Carson, J. G. (1993). Reading for writing: Cognitive perspectives. In J. G. Carson & I. Leki (Eds.), *Reading in the composition classroom: Second language perspectives* (pp. 85–104). Boston: Heinle & Heinle.

Carson, J. G. (2001). A task analysis of reading and writing in academic contexts. In D. Belcher & A. Hirvela (Eds.), *Linking literacies: Perspectives on L2 reading-writing connections* (pp. 48–83). Ann Arbor: University of Michigan Press.

Carson, J. G., Carrell, P. L., Silberstein, S., Kroll, B., & Kuehn, P. A. (1990). Reading-writing relationships in first and second language. *TESOL Quarterly, 24,* 245–266.

Carson, J. G., Chase, N. D., Gibson, S. U., & Hargrove, M. F. (1992). Literacy demands of the undergraduate curriculum. *Reading Research and Instruction, 31*(4), 25–50.

Carson, J. G., & Kuehn, P. A. (1992). Evidence of transfer and loss in developing second language writers. *Language Learning, 42,* 157–182.

Carson, J. G., & Leki, I. (1993a). Introduction. In J. G. Carson & I. Leki (Eds.), *Reading in the composition classroom: Second language perspectives* (pp. 1–7). Boston: Heinle & Heinle.

Carson, J. G., & Leki, I. (Eds.). (1993b). *Reading in the composition classroom: Second language perspectives.* Boston: Heinle & Heinle.

Carson, J. G., & Nelson, G. (1994). Writing groups: Cross-cultural issues. *Journal of Second Language Writing, 3,* 17–30.

Carson, J. G., & Nelson, G. (1996). Chinese students' perceptions of ESL peer response group interaction. *Journal of Second Language Writing, 5,* 1–20.

Carter, M. (1990). The idea of expertise: An exploration of cognitive and social dimensions of writing. *College Composition and Communication, 41,* 265–286.

Casanave, C. P. (1992). Cultural diversity and socialization: A case study of a Hispanic woman in a doctoral program in sociology. In D. E. Murray (Ed.), *Diversity as resource: Redefining cultural literacy* (pp. 148–182). Alexandria, VA: TESOL.

Casanave, C. P. (1995). Local interactions: Constructing contexts for composing in a graduate sociology program. In D. Belcher & G. Braine (Eds.), *Academic writing in a second language: Essays on research and pedagogy* (pp. 83–110). Norwood, NJ: Ablex.

Casanave, C. P., & Hubbard, P. (1992). The writing assignments and writing problems of doctoral students: Faculty perceptions, pedagogical issues, and needed research. *English for Specific Purposes, 11,* 33–49.

Cho, K. S., & Krashen, S. (1994). Acquisition of vocabulary from the Sweet Valley Kids series: Adult ESL acquisition. *Journal of Reading, 37,* 662–667.

Cho, K. S., & Krashen, S. (1995a). From *Sweet Valley* to Harlequins in one year. *California English, 1,* 18–19.

Cho, K. S., & Krashen, S. (1995b). Becoming a dragon: Progress in English as a second language through narrow free voluntary reading. *California Reader, 29,* 9–10.

Connor, U. (1996). *Contrastive rhetoric: Cross-cultural aspects of second-language writing.* Cambridge: Cambridge University Press.

Connor, U., & Kaplan, R. B. (Eds.) (1987). *Writing across languages: Analysis of L2 text.* Reading, MA: Addison-Wesley.

Connor, U., & Kramer, M. G. (1995). Writing from sources: Case studies of graduate students in business management. In D. Belcher & G. Braine (Eds.), *Academic writing in a second language: Essays on research and pedagogy* (pp. 155–182). Norwood, NJ: Ablex.

Connor, U., & Mayberry, S. (1996). Learning discipline-specific academic writing: A case study of a Finnish graduate student in the United States. In E. Ventola & A. Mauranen (Eds.), *Academic writing: Intercultural and textual issues* (pp. 231–253). Amsterdam: John Benjamins.

Constantino, R., Lee, S. Y., Cho, K. S., & Krashen, S. (1997). Free voluntary reading as a predictor of TOEFL scores. *Applied Language Learning, 8,* 111–118.

Costello, J. (1990). Promoting literacy through literature: Reading and writing in ESL composition. *Journal of Basic Writing, 9,* 20–30.

Culler, J. (1980). Prolegomena to a theory of reading. In S. Suleiman & I. Crosman (Eds.), *The reader in the text: Essays on audience and interpretation* (pp. 46–66). Princeton: Princeton University Press.

Culler, J. (1982). *On deconstruction: Theory and criticism after structuralism.* Ithaca, NY: Cornell University Press.

Cumming, A. (1989). Writing expertise and second language proficiency. *Language Learning, 39,* 81–141.

Cumming, A. (1990). Metalinguistic and ideational thinking in second language composing. *Written Communication, 7,* 482–511.

Cummins, J. (1979). Linguistic interdependence and the educational development of bilingual children. *Review of Educational Research, 49,* 222–251.

Cummins, J. (1980). The cross-lingual dimensions of language proficiency: Implications for bilingual education and the optimal age issue. *TESOL Quarterly, 14,* 175–187.

Cummins, J. (1984). *Bilingualism and special education: Issues in assessment and pedagogy.* Clevedon, Avon: Multilingual Matters.

Custodio, B., & Sutton, M. J. (1998). Literature-based ESL for secondary students. *TESOL Journal, 7*(5), 19–23.

Day, R. R., & Bamford, J. (1998). *Extensive reading in the second language classroom.* Cambridge: Cambridge University Press.

Deckert, G. D. (1993). Perspectives on plagiarism from ESL students in Hong Kong. *Journal of Second Language Writing, 2,* 131–148.

Devine, J. (1993). The role of metacognition in second language reading and writing. In J. G. Carson & I. Leki (Eds.), *Reading in the composition classroom: Second language perspectives* (pp. 105–127). Boston: Heinle & Heinle.

Dupuy, B., Tse, L., & Cook, T. (1996). Bringing students into the classroom: First steps in turning college-level ESL students into readers. *TESOL Journal, 5*(4), 10–16.

Eco, U. (1984). *The role of the reader: Explorations in the semiotics of texts.* Bloomington: Indiana University Press.

Ede, L., & Lunsford, A. (1990). *Singular texts/plural authors.* Carbondale: Southern Illinois University Press.

Eisterhold, J. (1990). Reading-writing connections: Toward a description for second language learners. In B. Kroll (Ed.), *Second language writing: Research insights for the classroom* (pp. 88–101). New York: Cambridge University Press.

Elley, W. B. (1991). Acquiring literacy in a second language: The effect of book-based programs. *Language Learning, 41,* 375–411.

Emig, J. (1977). Writing as a mode of learning. *College Composition and Communication, 27,* 122–128.

Eskey, D. E. (1993). Reading and writing as both cognitive process and social behavior. In J. G. Carson & I. Leki (Eds.), *Reading in the composition classroom: Second language perspectives* (pp. 221–233). Boston: Heinle & Heinle.

Eskey, D. E., & Grabe, W. (1988). Interactive models for second language reading: Perspectives on instruction. In P. L. Carrell, J. Devine, & D. E. Eskey (Eds.), *Interactive approaches to second language reading* (pp. 223–238). Cambridge: Cambridge University Press.

Faust, M. (2000). Reconstructing familiar metaphors: John Dewey and Louise Rosenblatt on literary art as experience. *Research in the Teaching of English, 35,* 9–34.

Ferris, D., & Hedgcock, J. (1998). *Teaching ESL composition: Purpose, process, and practice.* Mahwah, NJ: Lawrence Erlbaum.

Fish, S. (1980). *Is there a text in this class? The authority of interpretive communities.* Cambridge: Harvard University Press.

Flahive, D. E., & Bailey, N. H. (1993). Exploring reading/writing relationships in adult second language learners. In J. G. Carson & I. Leki (Eds.), *Reading in the composition classroom: Second language perspectives* (pp. 128–140). Boston: Heinle & Heinle.

Flesch, R. (1955). *Why Johnny can't read—and what you can do about it.* New York: Harper & Brothers.

Flesch, R. (1981). *Why Johnny still can't read: A new look at the scandal of our schools.* New York: Harper & Row.

Flowerdew, J., & Peacock, M. (Eds.) (2001). *Research perspectives on English for academic purposes.* Cambridge: Cambridge University Press.

Floyd, P., & Carrell, P. L. (1987). Effects on ESL reading of teaching cultural content schemata. *Language Learning, 37,* 89–108.

Flynn, E. (1982). Reconciling readers and texts. In T. Fulwiler & A. Young (Eds.), *Language connections: Writing and reading across the curriculum* (pp. 139–152). Urbana, IL: NCTE.

Fowler, R. (1971). *The languages of literature.* London: Routledge and Kegan Paul.

Fox, H. (1994). *Listening to the world: Cultural issues in academic writing.* Urbana, IL: NCTE.

Franklin, E. (Ed.). (1999). *Reading and writing in more than one language: Lessons for teachers.* Alexandria, VA: TESOL.

Freund, E. (1987). *The return of the reader: Reader-response criticism.* London: Methuen.

Friedlander, A. (1990). Composing in English: Effects of a first language on writing in English as a second language. In B. Kroll (Ed.), *Second language writing: Research insights for the classroom* (pp. 109–125). Cambridge: Cambridge University Press.

Fulwiler, T. (1987). *The journal book.* Portsmouth, NH: Boynton/Cook Heinemann.

Gage, J. (1986). Why write? In A. R. Petrosky & D. Bartholomae (Eds.), *The teaching of writing: Eighty-fifth yearbook of the National Society for the Study of Education* (Part 2, pp. 8–29). Chicago: NSSE.

Gajdusek, L. (1988). Toward wider use of literature in ESL: Why and how. *TESOL Quarterly, 22,* 227–257.

Gardner, S., & Fulwiler, T. (Eds.). (1999). *The journal book for teachers of at-risk college writers.* Portsmouth, NH: Boynton/Cook Heinemann.

Geisler, C. (1995). Writing and learning at cross purposes in the academy. In J. Petraglia (Ed.), *Reconceiving writing, rethinking writing instruction* (pp. 101–120). Mahwah, NJ: Lawrence Erlbaum.

Gergits, J. M. & Schramer, J. J. (1994). The collaborative classroom as a site of difference. *Journal of Advanced Composition, 14,* 187–202.

Geva, E., & Ryan, E. B. (1993). Linguistic and cognitive correlates of academic skills in first and second languages. *Language Learning, 43,* 5–42.

Goodman, K. (1968). The psycholinguistic nature of the reading process. In K. Goodman (Ed.), *The psycholinguistic nature of the reading process* (pp. 15–26). Detroit: Wayne State University Press.

Grabe, W. (2001). Reading-writing relations: Theoretical perspectives and instructional practices. In D. Belcher & A. Hirvela (Eds.), *Linking literacies: Perspectives on L2 reading-writing connections* (pp. 15–47). Ann Arbor: University of Michigan Press.

Grabe, W., & Kaplan, R. B. (1996). *Theory and practice of writing*. London: Longman.

Gradwohl Nash, J., Schumacher, G. M., & Carlson, B. W. (1993). Writing from sources: A structure-mapping model. *Journal of Educational Psychology 85,* 159–170.

Greene, S. (1993). Exploring the relationship between authorship and reading. In A. M. Penrose & M. M. Sitko (Eds.), *Hearing ourselves think: Cognitive research in the college writing classroom* (pp. 33–51). New York: Oxford University Press.

Haas, C. (1989). "Seeing on the screen isn't really seeing it": Computer writers' reading problems. In G. E. Hawisher & C. L. Selfe (Eds.), *Critical perspectives on computers and composition instruction* (pp. 16–29). New York: Teachers College Press.

Haas, C., & Flower, L. (1988). Rhetorical reading strategies and the construction of meaning. *College Composition and Communication, 39,* 167–183.

Haas, C., & Hayes, J. R. (1986). What did I just say? Reading problems in writing with the machine. *Research in the Teaching of English, 20,* 22–35.

Hall, C. (1990). Managing the complexity of revising across languages. *TESOL Quarterly, 24,* 43–60.

Hansen, J. (1987). *When writers read*. Portsmouth, NH: Heinemann.

Harklau, L. (2000). From the "good kids" to the "worst": Representations of English language learners across educational settings. *TESOL Quarterly, 34,* 35–67.

Hedgcock, J., & Atkinson, D. (1993). Differing reading-writing relationships in L1 and L2 literacy development? *TESOL Quarterly, 27,* 329–333.

Hedgcock, J., & Lefkowitz, N. (1992). Collaborative oral/aural revision in foreign language writing instruction. *Modern Language Journal, 80,* 287–308.

Herrington, A. (1981). Writing to learn: Writing across the disciplines. *College English, 43,* 379–387.

Hirvela, A. (1999a). Teaching immigrants in the college writing classroom. In M. H. Kells & V. Balester (Eds.), *Attending to the margins* (pp. 150–164). Portsmouth, NH: Boynton/Cook Heinemann.

Hirvela, A. (1999b). Collaborative writing instruction and communities of readers and writers. *TESOL Journal, 8*(2), 7–12.

Hirvela, A. (2001). Connecting reading and writing through literature. In D. Belcher & A. Hirvela (Eds.), *Linking literacies: Perspectives on L2 read-*

ing-writing connections (pp. 109–134). Ann Arbor: University of Michigan Press.

Hoekje, B. (1993–1994). Group work, the teacher's role, and the student-centered classroom. *TESOL Journal, 3*(2), 4–6.

Howard, R. M. (1993). A plagiarism *Pentimento. Journal of Teaching Writing, 11,* 233– 246.

Howard, R. M. (1995). Plagiarisms, authorships, and the academic death penalty. *College English, 57,* 788–806.

Horowitz, D. (1986). What professors actually require: Academic tasks for the ESL classroom. *TESOL Quarterly, 20,* 445–462.

Hudelson, S. (1989). *Write On: Children writing in ESL.* Englewood Cliffs, NJ: Center for Applied Linguistics and Prentice Hall Regents.

Hudelson, S. (1999). Evaluating reading, valuing the reader. In E. Franklin (Ed.), *Reading and writing in more than one language: Lessons for teachers* (pp. 81–94). Alexandria, VA: TESOL.

Hunt, R. A. (1985). Reading as writing: Meaning-making and sentence combining. In D. A. Daiker, A. Kerek, & M. Morenberg (Eds.), *Sentence combining: A rhetorical perspective* (pp. 159–174). Carbondale: Southern Illinois University Press.

Huss, R. L. (1995). Young children becoming literate in English as a second language. *TESOL Quarterly, 29,* 767–774.

Hutchinson, T., & Waters, A. (1987). *English for specific purposes: A learning-centred approach.* Cambridge: Cambridge University Press.

Iser, W. (1974). *The implied reader: Patterns of communication in prose fiction from Bunyan to Beckett.* Baltimore: Johns Hopkins University Press.

Iser, W. (1978). *The act of reading: A theory of aesthetic response.* Baltimore: Johns Hopkins University Press.

Janopoulos, M. (1986). The relationship of pleasure reading and second language writing proficiency. *TESOL Quarterly, 20,* 763–768.

Jenkins, S., Jordan, M. K., & Weiland, P. O. (1993). The role of writing in graduate engineering education: A survey of faculty beliefs and practices. *English for Specific Purposes, 12,* 51–67.

Johns, A. M. (1981). Necessary English: A faculty survey. *TESOL Quarterly, 15,* 51–58.

Johns, A. M. (1985). Summary protocols of "underprepared" and "adept" university students: Replications and distortions of the original. *Language Learning, 35,* 495–513.

Johns, A. M. (1991). Interpreting an English competency examination: The frustrations of an ESL science student. *Written Communication, 8,* 379–401.

Johns, A. M. (1992). Toward developing a cultural repertoire: A case study of a Lao college freshman. In D. E. Murray (Ed.), *Diversity as resource: Redefining cultural literacy* (pp. 183–201). Alexandria, VA: TESOL.

Johns, A. M. (1993). Reading and writing tasks in English for academic purposes classes: Products, processes, and resources. In J. G. Carson and I. Leki (Eds.), *Reading in the composition classroom: Second language perspectives* (pp. 274–285). Boston: Heinle & Heinle.

Johns, A. M. (1995). Teaching classroom and authentic genres: Initiating students into academic cultures and discourses. In D. Belcher & G. Braine (Eds.), *Academic writing in a second language: Essays on research and pedagogy* (pp. 277–291). Norwood, NJ: Ablex.

Johns, A. M. (1997). *Text, role, and context.* Cambridge: Cambridge University Press.

Johns, A. M., & Mayes, P. (1990). An analysis of summary protocols of university ESL students. *Applied Linguistics, 11,* 253–271.

Johnson, P. (1982). Effects on comprehension of building background knowledge. *TESOL Quarterly, 16,* 503–516.

Jordan, R. R. (1997). *English for academic purposes: A guide and resource book for teachers.* Cambridge: Cambridge University Press.

Kasper, L. F. (Ed.) (2000). *Content-based college ESL instruction.* Mahwah, NJ: Lawrence Erlbaum.

Kauffman, R. A. (1996). Writing to read and reading to write: Teaching literature in the foreign language classroom. *Foreign Language Annals, 29,* 396–402.

Kennedy, M. L., Kennedy, W. J., & Smith, H. M. (2000). *Writing in the disciplines: A reader for writers.* Upper Saddle River, NJ: Prentice Hall.

Kern, R., & Warschauer, M. (2000). Introduction: Theory and practice of network-based language teaching. In M. Warschauer & R. Kern (Eds.), *Network-based language teaching: Concepts and practice* (pp. 1–19). Cambridge: Cambridge University Press.

Kim, H., & Krashen, S. (1997). Why don't language acquirers take advantage of the power of reading? *TESOL Journal, 6*(3), 26–29.

Kinsella, K. (1996). Designing group work that supports and enhances diverse classroom work styles. *TESOL Journal, 6*(3), 24–30.

Kirkland, M. R., & Saunders, M. A. P. (1991). Maximizing student performance in summary writing: Managing cognitive load. *TESOL Quarterly, 25,* 105–121.

Kobayashi, H., & Rinnert, C. (1992). Effects of first language on second language writing: Translation versus direct composition. *Language Learning, 42,* 183–215.

Krashen, S. (1984). *Writing: Research, theory, and applications.* Oxford, UK: Pergamon.

Krashen, S. (1993). *The power of reading.* Englewood, CA: Libraries Unlimited.

Kroll, B. (1993). Teaching writing IS teaching reading: Training the new teacher of ESL composition. In J. G. Carson & I. Leki (Eds.), *Reading in the composition classroom: Second language perspectives* (pp. 61–81). Boston: Heinle & Heinle.

Kucan, L., & Beck, I. L. (1997). Thinking aloud and reading comprehension research: Inquiry, instruction, and social interaction. *Review of Educational Research, 67,* 271–299.

Kutz, E., Groden, S. Q., & Zamel, V. (1993). *The discovery of competence: Teaching and learning with diverse student writers.* Portsmouth, NH: Boynton/Cook.

Lam, W. S. E. (2000). L2 literacy and the design of the self: A case study of a teenager writing on the Internet. *TESOL Quarterly, 34,* 457–482.

Langer, J. A. (1986). Learning through writing: Study skills in the content areas. *Journal of Reading, 29,* 400–406.

Lay, N. D. (1995). Response journals in the ESL classroom: Windows to the world. *Teaching English in the Two-Year College, 16,* 38–44.

Leki, I. (1991). Building expertise through sequenced writing assignments. *TESOL Journal, 1*(2), 19–23.

Leki, I. (1992). *Understanding ESL writers: A guide for teachers.* Portsmouth, NH: Boynton/Cook.

Leki, I. (1993). Reciprocal themes in ESL reading and writing. In J. G. Carson & I. Leki (Eds.), *Reading in the composition classroom: Second language perspectives* (pp. 9–32). Boston: Heinle & Heinle.

Leki, I. (1999). "Pretty much screwed up": Ill-served needs of a permanent resident. In L. Harklau, K. M. Losey, & M. Siegal (Eds.), *Generation 1.5 meets college composition: Issues in the teaching of writing to U.S.-educated learners of ESL* (pp. 17–43). Mahwah, NJ: Lawrence Erlbaum.

Lent, R. (1993). "I can relate to that . . .": Reading and responding in the writing classroom. *College Composition and Communication, 44,* 232–240.

Leu, D. F. (2000). Literacy and technology: Deictic consequences for literacy education in an information age. In M. L. Kamil, P. B. Mosenthal, P.

D. Pearson, & R. Barr (Eds.), *Handbook of Reading Research,* Vol. 3 (pp. 743–770). Mahwah, NJ: Lawrence Erlbaum.

Li, S., & Munby, H. (1996). Metacognitive strategies in second language academic reading: A qualitative investigation. *English for Specific Purposes, 15,* 199–216.

Liu, J. (1998). Peer review with the instructor: Seeking alternatives in ESL writing. In J. Richards (Ed.), *Teaching in action: Case studies from second language classrooms* (pp. 237–240). Alexandria, VA: TESOL.

Liu, J., & Hansen, J. G. (2002). *Peer response in second language writing classrooms.* Ann Arbor: University of Michigan Press.

Lunsford, A. A. (1978). What we know—and don't know—about remedial writing. *College Composition and Communication, 29,* 47–52.

Macguire, M. (1999). A bilingual child's choices and voices: Lessons in noticing, listening, and understanding. In E. Franklin (Ed.), *Reading and writing in more than one language* (pp. 115–149). Alexandria, VA: TESOL.

Many, J. E., Fyfe, R., Lewis, G., & Mitchell, E. (1996). Traversing the topical landscape: Exploring students' self-directed reading-writing-research process. *Reading Research Quarterly, 31,* 12–35.

Marshall, J. D. (1987). The effects of writing on students' understanding of literary texts. *Research in the Teaching of English, 21,* 30–63.

Matsuda, P. K. (2001). Reexamining audiolingualism: On the genesis of reading and writing in L2 studies. In D. Belcher & A. Hirvela (Eds.), *Linking literacies: Perspectives on L2 reading-writing connections* (pp. 84–105). Ann Arbor: University of Michigan Press.

McGinley, W., & Tierney, R. J. (1989). Traversing the topical landscape: Reading and writing as ways of knowing. *Written Communication, 6,* 243–269.

McLeod, S., & Maimon, E. (2000). Clearing the air: WAC myths and realities. *College English, 62,* 573–583.

Mlynarczyk, R. W. (1998). *Conversations of the mind: The uses of journal writing for second-language learners.* Mahwah, NJ: Lawrence Erlbaum.

Murray, A., Parrish, J., & Salvatori, M. (1998, April). *To rewrite the text I am reading: Pedagogies of annotation.* Paper presented at the Conference on College Composition and Communication, Chicago, IL.

Murray, D. M. (1982). Teaching the other self: The writer's first reader. *College Composition and Communication, 33,* 140–147.

Nelson, G. L, & Carson, J. G. (1998). ESL students' perceptions of effectiveness in peer response groups. *Journal of Second Language Writing, 7,* 113–132.

Nelson, G., & Murphy, J. (1992). An L2 writing group: Task and social dimensions. *Journal of Second Language Writing, 1,* 171–193.

Nelson, G., & Murphy, J. (1992–1993). Writing groups and the less proficient ESL student. *TESOL Journal, 2*(2), 23–25.

Nelson, G., & Murphy, J. (1993). Peer response groups: Do L2 writers use peer comments in revising their drafts? *TESOL Quarterly, 27,* 135–142.

Nelson, N. (1998). Reading and writing contextualized. In N. Nelson & R. C. Calfee (Eds.), *The reading-writing connection: Ninety-seventh yearbook of the National Society for the Study of Education* (Part 2, pp. 266–285). Chicago: University of Chicago Press.

Newell, G. E. (1984). Learning from writing in two content areas: A case study/protocol analysis. *Research in the Teaching of English, 18,* 265–287.

Newell, G. E. (1998). "How much are we the wiser?": Continuity and change in writing and learning in the content areas. In N. Nelson & R. C. Calfee (Eds.), *The reading-writing connection: Ninety-seventh yearbook of the National Society for the Study of Education* (Part 2, pp. 178–202). Chicago: University of Chicago Press.

Newell, G. E., Suszynski, K., & Weingart, R. (1989). The effects of writing in a reader-based and text-based mode on students' understanding of two short stories. *Journal of Reading Behavior, 21,* 37–57.

Newell, G. E., & Winograd, P. (1989). The effects of writing for learning from expository text. *Written Communication, 6,* 196–217.

Newell, G. E., & Winograd, P. (1995). Writing about and learning from history texts: The effects of task and academic ability. *Research in the Teaching of English, 29,* 133–163.

Newkirk, T. (1986). Background and introduction. In T. Newkirk (Ed.), *Only connect: Uniting reading and writing* (pp. 1–8). Upper Montclair, NJ: Boynton/Cook.

Odell, L. (1980). The process of writing and the process of learning. *College Composition and Communication, 3,* 42–50.

Osburne, A. G., and Mulling, S. S. (1998). *Writing together: A project for team research.* Ann Arbor: University of Michigan Press.

Ostler, S. E. (1980). A survey of academic needs for advanced ESL. *TESOL Quarterly, 14,* 489–502.

Panetta, C. G. (Ed.). (2001). *Contrastive rhetoric revisited and redefined.* Mahwah, NJ: Lawrence Erlbaum.

Panferov, S. (2002). *Exploring the literacy development of Russian and Somali ESL learners: A collaborative ethnography.* Unpublished doctoral dissertation, Ohio State University, Columbus.

Parry, K. (1996). Culture, literacy, and L2 reading. *TESOL Quarterly, 30,* 665–692.

Pecorari, D. (2001). Plagiarism and international students: How the English-speaking university responds. In D. Belcher & A. Hirvela (Eds.), *Linking literacies: Perspectives on L2 reading-writing connections* (pp. 229–245). Ann Arbor: University of Michigan Press.

Pennington, M. C., & Zhang, D. (1993). A survey of writing attitudes and activities of Chinese graduate students at a U.S. university. In M. N. Brock & L. Walters (Eds.), *Teaching composition around the Pacific rim: Politics and pedagogy* (pp. 75–89). Clevedon, Avon: Multilingual Matters.

Pennycook, A. (1994). The complex contexts of plagiarism: A reply to Deckert. *Journal of Second Language Writing, 3,* 277–284.

Pennycook, A. (1996). Borrowing others' words: Text, ownership, memory, and plagiarism. *TESOL Quarterly, 30,* 201–230.

Peregoy, S. F., & Boyle, O. F. (2001). *Reading, writing, & learning in ESL: A resource book for K–12 teachers.* New York: Longman.

Perfetti, C. A., & Zhang, S. (1996). What it means to learn to read. In M. F. Graves, P. van den Broek, & B. M. Taylor (Eds.), *The first R: Every child's right to read* (pp. 37– 61). New York: Teachers College Press.

Peritz, J. H. (1993). Making a place for the poetic in academic writing. *College Composition and Communication, 44,* 380–385.

Petersen, B. T. (1982). Writing about responses: A unified model of reading, interpretation, and composition. *College English, 44,* 459–468.

Petrosky, A. R. (1982). From story to essay: Reading and writing. *College Composition and Communication, 3,* 19–36.

Peyton, J. K. (Ed.). (1990). *Students and teachers writing together: Perspectives on journal writing.* Alexandria, VA: TESOL.

Peyton, J. K. & Reed, L. (1990). *Dialogue journal writing with nonnative English speakers: A handbook for teachers.* Alexandria, VA: TESOL.

Peyton, J. K., & Staton, J. (Eds.). (1991). *Writing our lives: Reflections on dialogue journal writing with adult learners of English.* Englewood Cliffs, NJ: Center for Applied Linguistics and Prentice Hall Regents.

Price, M. (2002). Beyond "Gotcha!": Situating plagiarism in policy and pedagogy. *College Composition and Communication, 54,* 88–115.

Probst, R. E. (1988). *Response and analysis: Teaching literature in junior and senior high school.* Portsmouth, NH: Boynton/Cook Heinemann.

Probst, R. E. (1990). Literature as exploration and the classroom. In E. J. Farrell & J. R. Squire (Eds.), *Transactions with literature: A fifty-year perspective* (pp. 27–38). Urbana, IL: NCTE.

Raimes, A. (1985). What unskilled ESL students do as they write: A classroom study of composing. *TESOL Quarterly, 19,* 229–258.

Raimes, A. (1987). Language proficiency, writing ability, and composing strategies: A study of ESL college student writers. *Language Learning, 37,* 439–468.

Reid, J. M. (1993a). Historical perspectives on writing and reading in the ESL classroom. In J.G. Carson & I. Leki (Eds.), *Reading in the composition classroom: Second language perspectives* (pp. 33–60). Boston: Heinle & Heinle.

Reid, J. M. (1993b). *Teaching ESL writing.* Englewood Cliffs, NJ: Prentice Hall Regents.

Reid, J. M., & Powers, J. (1993). Extending the benefits of small-group collaboration to the ESL writer. *TESOL Journal 2*(4), 25–32.

Reinking, D., & Bridwell-Bowles, L. (1991). Computers in reading and writing. In R. Barr, M. L. Kamil, P. B. Mosenthal, & P. D. Pearson (Eds.), *Handbook of reading research,* Vol. 2 (pp. 310–340). New York: Longman.

Reither, J. A., & Vipond, D. (1989). Writing as collaboration. *College English, 51,* 855–867.

Richards, I. A. (1929). *Practical criticism.* London: Routledge and Kegan Paul.

Rigg, P. (1991). Whole language in TESOL. *TESOL Quarterly, 25,* 521–542.

Ringbom, H. (1992). On L1 transfer in L2 comprehension and L2 production. *Language Learning, 42,* 85–112.

Rodby, J. (1992). *Appropriating literacy: Writing and reading in English as a second language.* Portsmouth, NH: Boynton/Cook Heinemann.

Rosenblatt, L. M. (1938/1976). *Literature as exploration.* New York: MLA.

Rosenblatt, L. M. (1978). *The reader, the text, the poem: The transactional theory of the literary work.* Carbondale: Southern Illinois University Press.

Salinger, J. D. (1951). *The catcher in the rye.* New York: Bantam Books.

Salvatori, M. (1996). Conversations with texts: Reading in the teaching of composition. *College English, 58,* 440–454.

Sarig, G. (1993). Composing a study summary: A reading/writing encounter. In J. G. Carson & I. Leki (Eds.), *Reading in the composition classroom: Second language perspectives* (pp. 161–182). Boston: Heinle & Heinle.

Schneider, M. L. (1990). Collaborative learning: A concept in search of a definition. *Issues in Writing, 2,* 26–39.

Schneider, M. L., & Fujishima, N. K. (1995). When practice doesn't make perfect: The case of a graduate ESL student. In D. Belcher & G. Braine (Eds.), *Academic writing in a second language: Essays on research and pedagogy* (pp. 3–22). Norwood, NJ: Ablex.

Scholes, R. (1985). *Textual power: Literary theory and the teaching of English.* New Haven: Yale University Press.

Schoonen, R., Hultsjin, J., & Bossers, B. (1998). Metacognitive and language-specific knowledge in native and foreign language reading comprehension: An empirical study among Dutch students in grades 6, 8, and 10. *Language Learning, 48,* 71–106.

Schumacher, G. M., & Gradwohl Nash, J. (1991). Conceptualizing and measuring knowledge change due to writing. *Research in the Teaching of English, 25,* 67–96.

Scollon, R. (1994). As a matter of fact: The changing ideology of authorship and responsibility in discourse. *World Englishes, 13,* 33–46.

Scollon, R. (1995). Plagiarism and ideology: Identity in intercultural discourse. *Language in Society, 24,* 1–28.

Selden, R. (1986). *Practicing theory and reading literature.* Lexington: University Press of Kentucky.

Selfe, C. L. (1986). Reading as a writing strategy: Two case studies. In B. T. Petersen (Ed.), *Convergences: Transactions in reading and writing* (pp. 46–63). Urbana, IL: NCTE.

Selfe, C. L. (1989). Redefining literacy: The multilayered grammars of composition. In G. E. Hawisher & C. L. Selfe (Eds.), *Critical perspectives on computers and composition instruction* (pp. 3–15). New York: Teachers College Press.

Shen, F. (1989). The classroom and the wider culture: Identity as a key to learning English composition. *College Composition and Communication, 40,* 459–466.

Sheridan, D. (1991). Changing business as usual: Reader response in the classroom. *College English, 53,* 804–814.

Shih, M. (1986). Content-based approaches to teaching academic writing. *TESOL Quarterly, 20,* 617–648.

Shirk, H. N. (1991). Hypertext and composition studies. In G. E. Hawisher & C. L. Selfe (Eds.), *Evolving perspectives on computers and composition: Questions for the 1990s* (pp. 177–202). Urbana, IL: NCTE.

Shulman, M. (1995). *Journeys through literature.* Ann Arbor: University of Michigan Press.

Sills, C. K. (1988). Interactive learning in the composition classroom. In J. Golub (Ed.), *Focus on collaborative learning* (pp. 21–28). Urbana, IL: NCTE.

Slatin, J. M. (1990). Reading hypertext: Order and coherence in a new medium. *College English, 52,* 870–883.

Smagorinsky, P. (1992). How reading model essays affects writers. In J. Irwin & M. A. Doyle (Eds.), *Reading/writing connections: Learning from research* (pp. 160–176). Newark, DE: International Reading Association.

Smagorinsky, P. (1997). Personal growth in social context: A high school senior's search for meaning in and through writing. *Written Communication, 14,* 63–105.

Smith, F. (1971). *Understanding reading: A psycholinguistic analysis of reading and learning to read.* New York: Holt, Rinehart, and Winston.

Smith, F. (1983). Reading like a writer. *Language Arts, 60,* 558–567.

Smoke, T. (1994). Writing as a means of learning. *College ESL, 4,* 1–11.

Snow, M. A. (1998). Trends and issues in content-based instruction. *Annual Review of Applied Linguistics, 18,* 243–267.

Snow, M. A., & Brinton, D. M. (1988). Content-based language instruction: Investigating the effectiveness of the adjunct model. *TESOL Quarterly, 22,* 553–574.

Soven, M. K. (1996). *Write to learn: A guide to writing across the curriculum.* Cincinnati: South-Western College Publishing.

Spack, R. (1985). Literature, reading, writing, and ESL: Bridging the gaps. *TESOL Quarterly, 19,* 703–725.

Spack, R. (1988). Initiating students into the academic discourse community: How far should we go? *TESOL Quarterly, 22,* 29–52.

Spack, R. (1990). *Guidelines: A cross-cultural reading/writing text.* New York: St. Martin's Press.

Spack, R. (1993). Student meets text, text meets student: Finding a way into academic discourse. In J. G. Carson & I. Leki (Eds.), *Reading in the com-*

position classroom: Second language perspectives (pp. 183–196). Boston: Heinle & Heinle.

Spack, R. (1994). *The international story.* New York: St. Martin's Press.

Spack, R. (1997). The acquisition of academic literacy in a second language. *Written Communication, 14,* 3–62.

Sternglass, M. (1993). Writing development as seen through longitudinal research: A case study exemplar. *Written Communication, 10,* 235–261.

Stotsky, S. (1983). Research on reading/writing relationships: A synthesis and suggested directions. *Language Arts, 60,* 627–642.

Stotsky, S. (1995). The uses and limitations of personal or personalized writing in writing theory, research, and instruction. *Reading Research Quarterly, 30,* 758–776.

Stubbs, M. (1986). *Educational linguistics.* Oxford: Basil Blackwell.

Swales, J. (1990). *Genre analysis: English in academic and research settings.* Cambridge: Cambridge University Press.

Taylor, I., & Taylor, M. M. (1995). *Writing and literacy in Chinese, Korean and Japanese.* Amsterdam: John Benjamins.

Thomson, J. (1993). Helping students control texts: Contemporary literary theory into classroom practice. In S. B. Straw & D. Bogdan (Eds.), *Constructive reading: Teaching beyond communication* (pp. 130–154). Portsmouth, NH: Boynton/Cook Heinemann.

Tierney, R. J. (1992). Ongoing research and new directions. In J. W. Irwin & M. A. Doyle (Eds.), *Reading/writing connections: Learning from research* (pp. 246–259). Newark, DE: International Reading Association.

Tierney, R. J., & Leys, M. (1986). What is the value of connecting reading and writing? In B. T. Petersen (Ed.), *Convergences: Transactions in reading and writing* (pp. 15–29). Urbana, IL: NCTE.

Tierney, R. J., & Pearson, P. D. (1983). Toward a composing model of reading. *Language Arts, 60,* 568–580.

Tierney, R. J., & Shanahan, T. (1991). Research on the reading-writing relationship: Interactions, transactions, and outcomes. In R. Barr, M. L. Kamil, P. B. Mosenthal, & P. D. Pearson (Eds.), *Handbook of reading research,* Vol. 2 (pp. 246–280). New York: Longman.

Tierney, R. J., Soter, A., O'Flahavan, J. F., & McGinley, W. (1989). The effects of reading and writing upon thinking critically. *Reading Research Quarterly, 24,* 134–173.

Trimbur, J. (1989). Consensus and difference in collaborative learning. *College English, 51,* 602–616.

Tsang, W. K. (1996). Comparing the effects of reading and writing on writing performance. *Applied Linguistics, 17,* 210–233.

Tuman, M. (1992). *Word perfect: Literacy in the computer age.* Pittsburgh: University of Pittsburgh Press.

Vacca, J. A. L., Vacca, R. T., & Gove, M.K. (1991). *Reading and learning to read.* New York: HarperCollins.

Vacca, R. T., & Linek, W. M. (1992). Writing to learn. In J.W. Irwin & M.A. Doyle (Eds.), *Reading/writing connections: Learning from research* (pp. 145–159). Newark, DE: International Reading Association.

Vandrick, S. (1997). Diaspora literature: A mirror for ESL students. *College ESL, 7,* 53–69.

Verhoeven, L. T. (1994). Transfer in bilingual development: The linguistic interdependence hypothesis revisited. *Language Learning, 44,* 381–415.

Walworth, M. (1990). Interactive teaching of reading: A model. In J. K. Peyton (Ed.), *Students and teachers writing together: Perspectives on journal writing* (pp. 35–47). Alexandria, VA: TESOL.

Warschauer, M. (1999). *Electronic literacies: Language, culture, and power in online education.* Mahwah, NJ: Lawrence Erlbaum.

Weissberg, R. (1998). Acquiring English syntax through journal writing. *College ESL, 8,* 1–22.

Whalen, K., & Menard, N. (1995). L1 and L2 writers' strategic and linguistic knowledge: A model of multiple-level discourse processing. *Language Learning, 45,* 381–418.

White, E. (1994). *Teaching and assessing writing* (2nd ed.). San Francisco: Jossey-Bass.

Widdowson, H. G. (1983). *Learning purpose and language use.* Oxford: Oxford University Press.

Wiesel, E. (1960). *Night.* New York: Bantam Books.

Zamel, V. (1983). The composing processes of advanced ESL students: Six case studies. *TESOL Quarterly, 17,* 165–187.

Zamel, V. (1992). Writing one's way into reading. *TESOL Quarterly, 26,* 463–485.

Zhang, S. (1995). Reexamining the affective advantage of peer feedback in the ESL writing class. *Journal of Second Language Writing, 4,* 209–222.

Zhu, W. (1995). Effects of training for peer response on students' comments and interaction. *Written Communication, 12,* 492–528.

Subject Index

Author Index